Management 4.0
Empowering Managers through Emerging Technologies

Edited by:
Prof. Anurag Singh
Dr Rubee Singh

Foreword by:
Prof. Himanshu Rai
(Director-IIM Indore)

First Published in January 2023

ISBN: 978-93-5704-605-3

BLUEROSE PUBLISHERS
www.BlueRoseONE.com
info@bluerosepublishers.com
+91 8882 898 898

Cover Design:
Muskan Sachdeva

Typographic Design:
Rohit

Distributed by: BlueRose, Amazon, Flipkart

Management 4.0: Empowering Managers through Emerging Technologies

Edited by

Prof. Anurag Singh

Dr Rubee Singh

Foreword by

Prof. Himanshu Rai

(Director- IIM Indore, India)

Prof. (Dr) Himanshu Rai
Director
Indian Institute of Management
Indore (MP) INDIA

Foreword

It's an opportune time to reflect on the various changes that have taken place in the industrial sector and its workforce throughout the world. Over the past 15 – 20 years, the working systems and various procedures have transformed towards a focus on digital technologies. And this new system of work will further enhance its boundaries. Now, the entire world is focusing towards a fourth industrial revolution, wherein there shall be lot of changes in work cultures and a demand for the knowledge needed to adopt these changes during the revolutions.

The motive is to enhance the capabilities of the work force to adopt the prospective changes likely to knock on the industry's doors over the next few decades. This book 'Management 4.0 : Empowering Managers through Emerging Technologies' will give a wide scope to future leaders and the workforce to understand the basics of the working culture likely to be in place after the fourth industrial revolution. The book will play a vital role in educating future leaders on how to adopt the required changes and to enhance their capabilities to meet future targets and expectations.

Keeping the future prospects in mind, I recommend this book not only for future leaders but even for students currently, to help them update their thoughts, and knowledge and to understand various possible changes likely to take place after the fourth industrial revolution.

Happy Reading....

Prof. (Dr) Himanshu Rai
Director
Indian Institute of Management
Indore (MP) INDIA

Acknowledgment

Heartfelt thanks to all the authors from India and abroad who have contributed in bringing out this book on a very generic and contemporary topic. We appreciate their academic orientation and intellectual equity. We further would like to convey our sincere thanks to Professor Himanshu Rai, Director, IIM Indore, India for his encouragement and constant support he has been gracious enough to write a foreword of this book which lucidly summarises its central theme apart from providing way forward for the present and the next generation of managers and leaders.

We will be feeling in our duty if we do not acknowledge the good and timely support of GLA University top management namely Honourable Chancellor Shri Narayan Das Agarwal Ji, Pro Chancellor Dr D S. Chauhan, Vice Chancellor Dr Phalguni Gupta, Pro Vice Chancellor Dr Anup Kumar Gupta, Dean Academics Dr Ashish Sharma, Registrar Shri Ashok Kumar Singh, CEO Mr Neeraj Agarwal and CFO Mr Vivek Agarwal.

Lastly, we are immensely thankful to Bluerose Publishers, New Delhi, for bringing out this publication in a very professional and timely manner.

Prof Anurag Singh

Dr Rubee Singh

Corresponding Editor: *Dr Rubee Singh, Institute of Business Management, GLA University, Mathura, U.P (India), (dr.rubeerajput@gmail.com)*

Preface

Over the past two decades, digital technologies have become more available and increasingly integral to most workplaces. This disruption intends to accelerate over the next two decades, transforming the workplace and the world. Management 4.0 seeks to understand what the Fourth Industrial Revolution (Industry 4.0) will mean for the management profession and what new skills and knowledge we need to embed in existing and future leaders. Management 4.0 will explore the future of management, seeking to engage across industries and organizations to understand what we need to do now to prepare current and next-generation leaders for the future. Management skills and practices are essential to improving the quality of work, enhancing organizational performance, and closing the productivity gap. The Fourth Industrial Revolution is characterized by the fusion of technologies, including Artificial Intelligence (AI), automation, and the Internet of Things. These emerging technologies will not replace managers, but they may fundamentally change the role of managers and lead to new management tools and practices.

In today's management environment, the concept of employee empowerment is becoming increasingly important, as are the potential impacts of emerging technologies on employee empowerment. Through the change that empowerment implies within a company, the article attempts to assess the role of Industry 4.0 as well as its application within that context. In our opinion, emerging technologies cannot be considered to "Empower" employees today because employee empowerment has become a conscious and highly political organizational choice. Rather, they should be considered a support tool that can facilitate empowerment, depending on the organizational context, specifically the four main organizational variables in the digital age; structure, culture, people, and tasks and procedures. A conceptual framework for the book is developed to describe the impact of emerging technologies on empowerment, which includes how these variables appear in different organizations. A concept of management known as empowering managers through emerging technologies is the idea that employees are more productive and happier if they are given information, resources, and opportunities at the same time as they are held accountable for their job outcomes. The management needs to realize that it is not possible for an organization to implement empowerment itself - instead, the management needs to create an environment that allows empowerment to happen.

So how does a manager set up this kind of environment where employees feel empowered?

New industries can be built and transformed by emerging technologies such as the Internet of Things, Artificial Intelligence, Robotics, Machine Learning, and Automation. The incumbent firms, despite their superior resources, often lose out to smaller competitors when it comes to the development of emerging technologies. We would like to mention an example of a book by Wharton on managing emerging technologies that provides insights, tools, and frameworks from leading business thinkers that are based on the research of Wharton's Emerging Technologies Management Research Program. One of the longest and broadest initiatives related to emerging technologies management is this pioneering industry-academic partnership, which was established in 1994.

It is the opinion of the editors that managing emerging technologies represents a "different game," as it requires a different set of management skills, frameworks, and strategies than those used by established firms to manage those technologies that are already established. In this book, experts from diverse fields examine key issues such as: "New technologies have transformed organizational performance, markets, businesses, and society at an ever-increasing rate, resulting in new technologies transforming society." Managing our way through this new terrain requires a better understanding of the road maps we need to use. For the first time, this book distills the insights gained from the program into a single volume, which is designed to help managers cope with this new set of challenges. The book provides valuable new models for thinking through these issues and provides critical insight that will prove invaluable for managing emerging technologies.

We hope this edited book will be capable to quench the thrust of the readers who are really interested in emerging technologies in the field of Management.

Editors
Prof. Anurag Singh
Dr Rubee Singh
Mathura, Jan/2023

A note from the editor's desk

Happy to write the editorial of this book which assimilates the point of views of future gazers. The edited book titled "Management 4.0: Empowering Managers through Emerging Technologies" consists of 15 contributory articles from India and abroad.

To understand Management 4.0, we need to revisit our understanding about Industry 4.0 which represents the 4th industrial revolution the world is all set to witness in the near future. Industry 4.0 is characterised by fusion and adoption of new age technologies, encompassing Artificial Intelligence (AI), Machine Learning (ML), Automation and Internet of Things (IoT), by the industries across the world. To elaborate, we will find a network of digital systems capable of monitoring inputs from multiple sources, along with an AI enabled environment where decisions about the outputs of goods and services will be automated. The integration of a digital system facilitated by the internet of things will also communicate information to other devices and systems to perform the actions as per the instruction. This ecosystem of Industry 4.0 is going to bring big disruptions and transformation of the workforce. Most of the current jobs which are repetitive in nature are going to be taken over by the machines. This will bring big churning in the job markets. This disruption will tank up many of the current existing jobs we see around. Trusting the ingenuity of the human race, newer jobs would emerge, although largely unknown at the present. These new jobs will require different kinds of higher order skills. Management 4.0 is in the process of evolution on the side-lines of Industry 4.0, seeking to understand and deduce what impact later will have on the current management practices that have evolved and curated over more than hundred years. The ecosystem of Industry 4.0 encompassing AI, ML, IoT, Industry 4.0, is bound to have a profound impact on the management practices.

Management 4.0 describes the skills and practices that managers and leaders will require to complement the ecosystem of Industry 4.0. Existing workforce is aging where a new set of younger lots are joining the labour force. Significant numbers of existing jobs will vanish fast making way for newer ones. In such an environment one of the key roles of managers and leaders will be retaining, retraining and reskilling the workforce to meet the challenges and exploit the opportunities that would emerge. To facilitate this education has to be a lifelong pursuit and educational institutions must focus on nurturing and grooming the students with the mindset of being lifelong learners. We could see that structural changes in mode and the curriculum of higher education institutions are going through a phase of transition. There is more focus on outcome-based learning and skill development apart from practical exposure through internships. The New Education Policy (NEP 2020) introduced in India is much in alignment with these emerging challenges and opportunities. Management 4.0 calls upon the managers and leaders to be the change driver. They need to be innovative and early adopters of Industry 4.0 technologies. Managers need to be empowered by identifying the skill and competencies requirements to meet the need of changing job requirements. Though there are a lot of grey areas as we are expecting to prepare a workforce for the jobs which are not yet present there. Sometimes we really wish for a crystal ball to find answers to such situations. But what is certain is that managers and the leaders who are quick in adopting the technologies of Industry 4.0, swift in skilling their workforce, in new and emerging technologies, leveraging the ecosystem of Industry 4.0 will be better equipped for the sustainable growth and development.

Editors
Prof. Anurag Singh
Dr Rubee Singh

Brief Profile of Editor's

About Prof. Anurag Singh

Prof. Anurag Singh is an academician and a visionary thought leader in its true sense. With his exceptional critical thinking skills, he has been contributing his best efforts to the development of different fields and particularly management and academics. Currently, Prof. Anurag Singh is holding the position of Director at the Institute of Business Management, GLA University, India, where he is a great support to more than 2,000 students and 100 teaching staff. He is also active as the Vice–President of the National Human Resource Development Network (NHRDN), Mathura Chapter. He has been on a great journey of exploring different fields and gaining a good amount of knowledge which he is achieving greatly so far.

Prof. Anurag Singh has a vast experience as an academician, previous to this Prof Singh served as Professor & Dean of Academics at the University of Sterling, RAK, UAE Campus & Dean of Academics at Jaipuria Institute of Management, Jaipur & Noida campus. Before this, he also served as Adjunct Faculty, at Regenesys Business School, Johannesburg, South Africa. Prof. Anurag Singh has always been a great support for the students who seek guidance in their careers and studies from him, as a career counselor and launcher, he has been doing a great job in enlightening students and shepherding them through the door of success. He has also contributed his best efforts as the content developer, he has been selected for the Swayamprabha project of the Government of India, as a resource person for developing an online Corporate Finance course which will be soon launched on various social media platforms.

Further, he has always been a part of various research activities, seminars, and initiatives taken on the global and national levels related to different academic and non-academic fields and issues that are important to be addressed from the welfare point of view. He is recognized as an Accomplished Academic Administrator, Researcher at International Academic Association. He has a proven track record for conducting different MDPs, FDPs, SDPs, Conferences, Workshops, and Seminars for corporates and academicians. He has 25 years of rich academic and corporate experience. He is well known Indian expert to handle academic qualities for inspection in Assurance of Learning, Internal Quality Assurance Committee (IQAC), NIRF Ranking, National (NBA) & International Accreditation (AACSB). He has been delivering great content which is been honoured by various reputed publications, magazines, and journals. His work is even been a part of many books.

Being an active speaker, he has been playing the role of facilitator, jury, and active participant in various forums and platforms organized to address various issues and enlighten people about different credible ideas beyond the general perception. He also has years of experience being a corporate trainer. He has successfully guided the human resource of Indian Oil Corporation, National Hydro Power Corporation Ltd. (NHPC), Maruti Suzuki India Ltd, National Fertilizers Ltd. (NFL), National Thermal Power Corporation Ltd. (NTPC) & Handlooms & Handicrafts Export Corporation of India Ltd. (HHEC) about various finance related issue that requires great precision to be handled. He has handled the position of Workshop Director for 7 high profile MDP for leading corporate houses (Maruti Suzuki, Tata Motors, TCI). He has showcased his leadership qualities by leading through academic collaboration & MOU with Universities, Institutions, and Business Houses from the front.

His work and contribution are appreciated by every reputed organization he has been a part of. He has majorly done an excellent job in the field of academics; he has supervised Ph.D. students and over 500 Masters students which shows his dexter and the leadership trait he possesses. He has recently won the Pan Jaipuria White Paper Competition - "Innovation in Pedagogy" award for his contribution to the field of Finance by Jaipuria Jaipur in 2020. He has received the prestigious fellowship "UKIERI Technical Leadership Program 2019-20" by AICTE & Dudley College, UK for completing a level 5 certificate from Chartered Management Institute, London, in Leadership and Management. He has completed his Ph. D. in Finance from Jamia Millia University, Delhi. He is Editor, Author, and reviewer in peer review journals. He has published articles, and book chapters in reputed magazines and journals at national and international levels.

About Dr Rubee Singh

Your profession is not enough valued until it is driven by a great vision to uplift a critical issue predominantly rooted in society. Dr Rubee Singh is one such professional academician who has not only contributed significantly to sharpening the career of her students but also has been recognized as a visionary thought leader who has re-established many norms in the field of management by many reputed universities throughout the world. she is not only an inspiration for other fellow academicians but also a true form of women empowerment.

Dr Singh has five years experience in academia as an Assistant Professor. Her career journey is highly practical and showcased her as a devoted academician and learner. She was a part of Dr Abdul Kalam Technical University, Lucknow from Nov 2017 to Nov, 2020. It has been an exhilarating experience, and She feels very fortunate to have had the chance to serve for her country as through being responsible towards her profession and being a support system for those who dream to bring a change for good just like her.

Currently, Dr Rubee Singh is an Assistant Professor at the Institute of Business Management, GLA University, India. She has a great history of being a dedicated learner herself and she always believed in doing things that can change the lives of millions which she is trying to achieve by spreading her knowledge and empowering people through it. She is a Post-Doctoral Researcher (D.Lit.) at Kumaun University, Nainital. Not only a professional academician, but she also has great experience being an excellent Editor, Author, Global Ambassador (Children's) & Social Activist. For her dedication, hard work, and knowledge she has been awarded Honorary Doctorate in Human Rights & Peace from Royal American University USA for her outstanding contribution to social work.

Recently awarded as Chartered Global Peace Building Professional (CGPP) by The George Washington University of Peace, USA, Dr Rubee Singh is striving her best to become a professional people looks forward to guidance and mentorship. She holds a Doctorate in HR from Noida International University, India. Dr Singh is a Managing Editor of IJARSH India. She is the National Secretary of the International Anti-Terrorism Movement (Youth Wing). She is a United Nations Volunteer and also a contributing author for Voices of Youth (UNICEF). Invited by WEPS Forum of UN Women to attend IWD'20 in New York USA. She is an honorary life member of the Women's Economic Forum. Her profile is filled with the knowledge and experience collected through years of hard work and learning. Dr Rubee Singh supports progressive thinking and motivates people to take initiative and believe in making dreams come true. With her constant efforts, you will always find her mentoring and guiding her students to achieve great heights in their life, that's why she is often called an enthusiastic dreamer.

Dr Singh is the National Record Holder in the India Book of Records 2020 & Asia Book of Records Holder for 2021. She has published more than 40 research articles in a few leading journals like the Journal of Modelling Management, emerald, including Scopus, SCI, and ABDC category, and has also authored 14 books. Many reputed Universities have recognized her as a thought leader by adding her book to the library, Ohio Christian University, University of California, Corporacion Universitaria Unisabanta, UMass Chan Medical School, Tunix Community College, USA, Dow University of Health Sciences, Pakistan, University of Port Harcourt, Nigeria are the few significant among them. Her book titled "Training & Development" was added to the MBA syllabus of "The Institute of Aeronautical Engineering" (Jawaharlal Nehru Technological University, Hyderabad.

She is working on a few projects along with senior bureaucrats while her one book was published with Dr Kalpana Goplanan, IAS, Additional Chief Secretary, Karnataka & one textbook with Dr Prateep Philip, IPS, DGP Tamilnadu. She has received more than 50 awards in different fields. Recently she was awarded the International Excellent Researcher Award 2021 by Saksham Society Jaipur. Her research interests are Digital HRM, Digital Innovation, Sustainable HRM, Circular Economy, Sustainability, and Industry 4.0/I.5, Corporate Social Responsibility & Artificial Intelligence. With all the knowledge that she has stored in her book, she is contributing to the change and upliftment in various fields of study. Her contribution to the management field is unparalleled. Moving forward at a great pace Dr Rubee Singh aims to initiate a big change in the world.

Contents

Chapter 1
Fusion of Indurty 4.0 Technologies with Management: A Step Towards Management 4.0

Shahbaz Khan

Institute of Business Management, GLA University, Mathura, U.P

Abstract

In the age of Industry 4.0, some advanced technologies such as the Internet of Things (IoT), big data analytics and Blockchain have the potential to transform the shape of various businesses and their related activities. These technologies have tremendous capabilities to achieve operational excellence as well as sustainability by lowering the processing time, up-gradation of value chain coordination, increasing process flexibility and green product diffusion and trust building. In order to adopt these smart technologies, the management needs to be aware of the potential of smart technologies and their advantage in their business domain. Therefore, this study explores the significant smart technologies and their application in various business domains. Several smart technologies could transform traditional management practices. However, this chapter only focuses on the six popular smart technologies that will assist managers, decision-makers and policy planners to make their decision-making more accurate and data-driven. These smart technologies include big data, Blockchain, the Industrial Internet of Things (IIoT), cloud computing, and virtual reality/augmented reality (VR/AR). Further, this study also identifies the relevant challenges to the adoption of these technologies and recommends some potential solutions. This study will help the managers to align their business process with the industry 4.0 principles. Further, the findings of this study assist managers to transform their existing management practices in management 4.0.

Keywords: Industry 4.0; Management 4.0; Smart Technologies; Sustainability; Data Driven Decision Making

1. Introduction

Digitalization, robotics and artificial intelligence have contributed to the emergence of Industry 4.0 in the manufacturing and service sectors (Matt et al., 2020; Sony & Naik, 2019). Through the application of digital technologies, the connectivity of physical and cybernetic surroundings is established (Liu & Xu, 2017). A socio-technical revolution has been brought about by the usage of technologies like artificial intelligence, cyber-physical systems, big data, and cloud computing, which have had a disruptive effect on management activities (Fareri et al., 2020; Sony et al., 2020). These disruptions force us to change the nature of current management practices and give birth to the concept of management 4.0. To ensure the usability and efficiency of digital technologies, digital transformation requires intrinsic management skills.

However, not all managers of industrial enterprises grasp the importance of digital transformation objectively in the modern business environment. Others view this as an innovation in digital marketing. Few recognize digital transformation as the foundation for sustained corporate growth. McKinsey & Company have defined digitization inside the enterprise. Industry 4.0 is a paradigm for the integrated utilization of human resources, physical items, and digital technologies at any time that is quick, inexpensive, and dependable. Using this methodology, however, is not as straightforward as it may appear; frequently, businesses that are not well-versed in digital technologies attempt to calculate the experience of digital transformation in their firm by any means possible.

In order to transform conventional management practices, digital transformation is required. This transformation is done with the help of industry 4.0 technologies and leads towards management 4.0. Haleem et al., (2022) proposed a comprehensive definition of Management 4.0 as: "Management 4.0 is creating and operationalizing a digital environment through the effective integration of Industry 4.0 technologies, data, and knowledge, enabling high coordination & control amongst the different activities and working personnel in business organisation to create and enhance value." In this definition, technologies associated with Industry 4.0, data and knowledge are highlighted. In order to adopt Management 4.0, these three components must be interconnected. By implementing industry 4.0 technologies, data can be collected and analyzed. Using data analysis, organizations can make the right decision based on the knowledge gained. Using this knowledge, production could become more autonomous and agile. The interplay between man and machine is fundamentally changed by Management 4.0. As a result of these technologies, people and processes can work together more efficiently and effectively. As a result, waste generation, mistakes, and operational inefficiencies are reduced, resulting in businesses becoming more efficient.

As a result of Management 4.0, businesses are approaching production differently, and as a result, human resources are reduced, primarily through automation. In human resource management, data transmission has also drastically improved efficiency and decision-making processes. Data could be secured and stored more easily on the blockchain network.

Technologies used in Management 4.0

The digital transformation of the business forces the managers to adopt industry 4.0 technologies that help them make the right decisions at the right time. These technologies include blockchain, big data analytics, IoT, IIoT and many more. Among these technologies, six popular technologies are shown in figure 1 and discussed as follows:

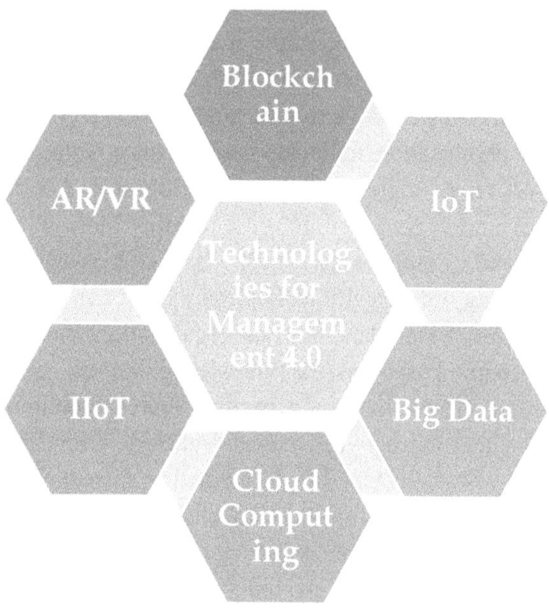

Figure 1: Technologies for management 4.0

1.4.1 Blockchain

Blockchain is a distributed ledger technology that uses cryptography to safeguard it and is used to store transaction histories. Every node on the blockchain system maintains a copy of all prior data and transactions made on that specific system. It is a decentralised system in this case since no single node is the owner. Other features of blockchain technology include auditability, immutability, smart contracts, peer-to-peer (P2P), traceability, and a reliable system of trust. Risius and Spohrer (2017) defined the BCT as "BCT refers to a fully distributed system for cryptographically capturing and storing a consistent, immutable, linear event log of transactions between networked actors. This is functionally similar to a distributed ledger that is consensually kept, updated, and validated by the parties involved in all the transactions within a network. In such a network, BCT enforces transparency and guarantees eventual, system-wide consensus on the validity of an entire history of transactions" From the earlier description, it is evident that BCT functions as a "digital logbook of transactions," with the essential characteristics of decentralisation, consistent, and immutable information sharing. As a result, the BCT is linked to transaction disintermediation, or the lack of a central authority to authenticate and certify transactions.

1.4.2 Internet of Things

Internet Society (ISOC) report refers to IoT as "The term IoT generally refers to scenarios where network connectivity and computing capability extend to objects, sensors and everyday items not normally considered computers, allowing these devices to generate, exchange and consume data with minimal human intervention". Furthermore, the IoT can also be defined as "a network of various physical items integrated with digital devices such as sensors, actuators, etc". These components are linked to gathering and sharing data. Moreover, communication is facilitated between networked devices or 'things,' systems, and services, enabling data exchange (Zhong et al., 2017; Kalsoom et al., 2020). The objective of the IoT idea is to enable 'things' in a system to do activities with higher precision, enhance their responsiveness, boost collaboration amongst entities in the system, and simultaneously enable learning. This is accomplished by providing the 'objects' in the system with the senses of sight, hearing, smell, touch, and speech.

1.4.3 Big Data

"National Institute for Standards and Technology (NIST)" of the USA defines Big Data as "advanced techniques that harness independent resources for building scalable data systems when the characteristics of the datasets require new architectures for efficient storage, manipulation, and analysis." The five Vs—velocity, veracity, volume, value, and variety—define big data. As the world has become increasingly data-centric, including in business, industry, services, and agriculture, it now has enormous importance in all areas. This data is analysed with big data analytics (BDA) which is the process of managing massive amounts of data. When the amount of data cannot be analysed by a single computer and there is a constant flow of information entering the system, and when the rate at which information is received is quick and variable, this technology is implemented (Bag et al., 2020; Ranjan, and Foropon, 2021). According to Bodrow (2017), Big Data is one of the most important enablers for the adoption of industry 4.0. Moreover, Fernandez-Miranda et al. (2017) state that Big data in an Industry 4.0 context involves the collection and comprehensive evaluation of data from a wide variety of sources, such as customers, operations, and sales, and that it will become a standard over time to support decision making and coordinate operations at optimal cost and performance. BDA may also be used to manufacture data from the firm and each of its suppliers to enhance the delivery information consumers get and to assess the performance of the suppliers.

1.4.4 Cloud computing

Cloud computing refers to the delivery of computational services via the internet through resources that are both scalable and visualized (Zhong et al., 2017; Li et al., 2020; Shukri et al., 2021). Toka (2013) defines Cloud computing as "an IT service model where computing services (both hardware and software) are delivered on-demand to customers over a self-service fashion, independent of device and location." At the request of clients, cloud computing offers computing services like storage, servers, networking, analytics, intelligence, and software over the internet ("the cloud"). NIST defines cloud computing as "a model for enabling ubiquitous, convenient, on-demand network access to a shared pool of configurable computing resources (e.g., networks, servers, storage, applications, and services) that can be rapidly provisioned and released with minimal management effort or service provider interaction". It is more affordable and offers good performance. Toka (2013) demonstrates that cloud computing enhances collaboration among stakeholders, indicating that cloud computing may be a useful tool in the SCM sector. Further, the author describes many supply chain management situations in which cloud computing may be utilised, including forecasting and planning, sourcing and procurement, and logistics.

1.5 Industrial Internet of things (IIoT)

Industrial Internet of things (IIoT) implies an industrial framework whereby a large number of devices or machines are connected and synchronised through the use of software tools and third-platform technologies in a machine-to-machine and Internet of Things (Hossain & Muhammad, 2016; Arnold et al., 2016; Khalil & Saeed, 2020). Krugh et al. (2017) characterise the IIoT as a linked production ecosystem that uses BD and consists of sensor data, machine learning, machine-to-machine communication, human-to-machine communication, and automation technologies. The IIoT is intended to enable root-cause investigation, detect inefficiencies, and provide business intelligence. According to Bisio et al. (2018), the IoT is the primary enabling technology for the fourth industrial revolution. IoT's primary purpose is the enhanced connection of electronic gadgets at any time and in any location.

1.6 Augmented Reality and Virtual reality

Augmented Reality and Virtual reality are reshaping the manufacturing domain. These technologies can be used in manufacturing assembly & quality control and assist employees in assembling the product with almost 100 percent accuracy. These technologies are also beneficial for training and maintenance during the manufacturing process. It will also reduce human errors, execution time, and downtime and increased productivity and speed (Dangelmaier et al., 2005; Novak-Marcincin et al., 2013; Dallasega et al., 2020). Industrial firms may profit from AR in the domains of production, shipping, maintenance, and training. AR is defined as the presentation of information and work instructions on wearable devices to aid workers in completing process tasks. Pick-by-vision, which is enabled by augmented reality in logistics, may boost the efficiency and speed of the picking operations for components and goods. Moreover, augmented reality may be used to integrate information directly into the workplace, therefore aiding workers by decreasing their cognitive load and enhancing the performance of various tasks (Strandhagen et al., 2017; Rejeb et al., 2020).

3.   Transformations through Management 4.0

Several transformations have been observed with the supportive practices of the management 4.0 scheme in different dimensions. Some significant highlights of changes through management 4.0, as reflected in Figure 2. The overall development of the industrial issues is named as; changes in technology with innovations like machine learning and artificial intelligence, issues of societal improvements, general work patterns transformations, leadership transformations with the provision of command and control of style and management throughout, and business transformations for the progressive development of industry practices as a whole.

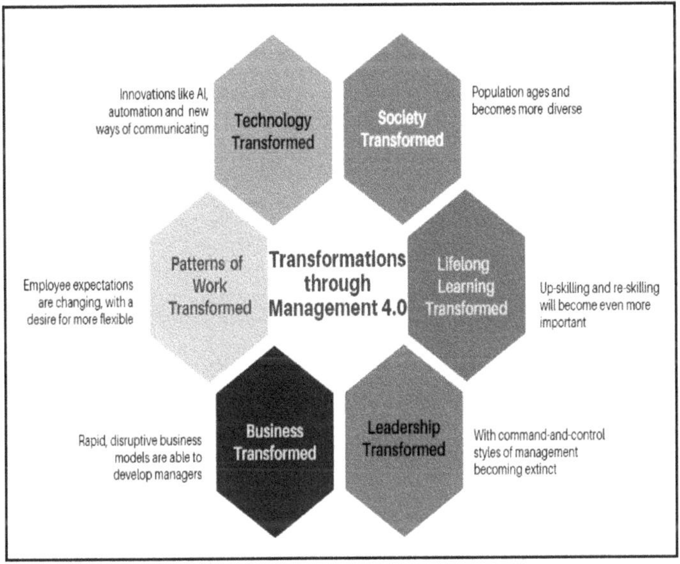

Figure 2: Transformations through Management 4.0
(Haleem et al., 2022)

4.   Management 4.0 Ecosystem

The management 4.0 Ecosystem entails the use of industry 4.0 technologies, digital capabilities, the unprecedented spread of IoT, and the extraordinary capacity to access data anywhere along the Supply Chain. These technologies support the complete visibility of the end-to-end supply chain from supplier to consumer. This visibility assists the stakeholders to access all the relevant information and make the right decision. The management 4.0 ecosystem consists of technological integration for planning, organising, controlling, procurement, logistics, manufacturing, recruitment, training, leadership and other aspects of management.

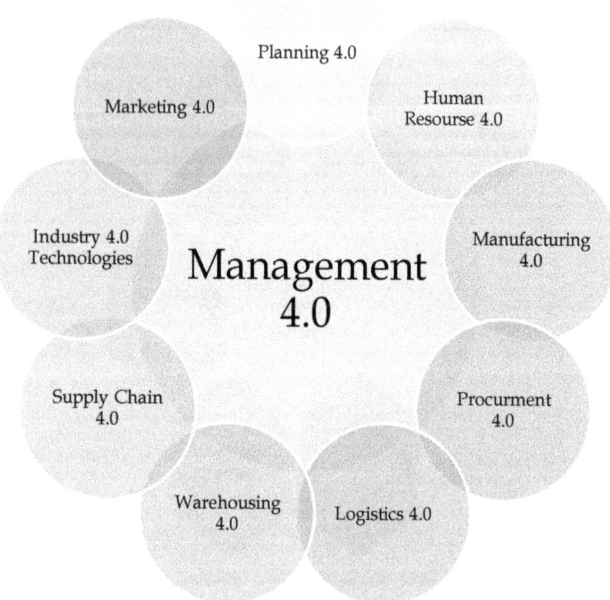

Figure 3: *Management 4.0 Ecosystem*

Several management functions are affected by the industry 4.0 technologies, for example, procurement 4.0. Companies can raise their competitiveness by integrating Industry 4.0 technologies and concepts into their procurement processes in order to cut costs and boost product quality by picking the most suitable raw material suppliers. In Procurement 4.0, valuable customer data can be utilised to improve the management of inventories, transportation flows, quality inspection, and warehouse needs, among other things (Geissbauer et al., 2016). AI, BDA, CC, IoT, horizontal and vertical Integration, and cybersecurity are the technical solutions suitable for Procurement 4.0. These technologies and ideas can be included in Procurement 4.0 for the real-time integration of data from suppliers, producers, distributors, and customers to minimise inventory costs, lead time, and supplier performance (Glas & Kleemann, 2016). AI is crucial for procurement because it can evaluate Data in real-time to discover opportunities and enhance decision-making. Companies may strengthen the relationship between buyers and suppliers and increase trust by enabling real-time access to information, which is supported by increased SC visibility.

Management 4.0 also focuses on manufacturing in addition to service sectors. Industry 4.0 targets the manufacturing segment of the value chain. Reduced product life cycles and consumer demand for customised products with shorter lead time need businesses to expedite product time-to-market while maintaining product quality in order to remain competitive. Production managers aim for high efficiency, effectiveness, process optimization, and shorter lead times at a lower cost and with less inventory on hand. This can be accomplished by implementing key I4.0 technologies and ideas, including IoT, BDA, CPS, AM, flexible automation, and industrial robotics.

Industry 4.0 affects SC dimensions and develops modern Logistics 4.0. The manufacturers' goal is to deliver the appropriate product to the right client at the right time in order to maintain a high level of customer satisfaction. There are several enabling technologies and ideas for Logistics 4.0, such as the Internet of Things (IoT), whose sensing, identifying, locating, processing, and acting capabilities are extremely significant for logistics. As the virtual and physical worlds converge, it is increasingly difficult to take action on anything not specified in the SC. RFID can be used to confirm that items "exist" in the system, and it provides a straightforward means of identifying the correct objects at the correct time and location. In transportation and logistics, IoT can deliver near-perfect orders, shipping, receiving, and inventory accuracy, as well as expedited order fulfilment. The IoT enhances SC visibility and enables firms to communicate information in real-time, connect all SC operations, and optimise and enhance the transparency of logistics processes.

Warehouse management or Warehousing 4.0 is an essential component of the SC. In Warehousing 4.0, production, warehouse transportation technologies, warehouse management systems, and manufacturing must all be considered together (Lerher, 2018). Industry 4.0 technologies and concepts, including as IoT, AI, AR, CPS, BD, CC, and autonomous vehicles, are key to Warehousing 4.0 technologies and concepts. Adopting these techniques and ideas leads to the optimal, cost-effective management of inventory levels. Manufacturers must be responsive to consumer demands, thus their inventories must be stocked with the appropriate raw materials and finished items to meet those demands. Horizontal integration with customers and suppliers yields more precise data for optimal warehouse resource utilisation. AR enables real-time user interaction with things and digital devices, and it can be applied to warehouse operations.

5. Conclusion

This chapter highlights the application of industry 4.0 technologies in management and reviews the emerging concepts of management 4.0. This work seeks to investigate the present state of the art in Industry 4.0 technologies in the management domain. Further, some popular technologies such as IoT, IIoT, AR/VR, big data and blockchain are discussed. These technologies help managers to make better and faster decisions for several management processes, including, planning, procurement, logistics, marketing and warehousing. In addition to this, the transformations through Management 4.0 are also highlighted. These transformations include leadership, societal, work culture and learning. The last section of this chapter focuses on the management 4.0 ecosystem, conceptualised for a better understanding of its implementations. The findings of this study will assist managers, decision makers and policy planners to make their decision-making more accurate and data driven.

References

Arnold, B., Salman Abdul Baset, Paolo Dettori, M. Kalantar, I. I. Mohomed, S. J. Nadgowda, M. Sabath et al. "Building the IBM Containers cloud service." *IBM Journal of Research and Development* 60, no. 2-3 (2016): 9-1.

Bag, S., Wood, L. C., Mangla, S. K., & Luthra, S. (2020b). Procurement 4.0 and its implications on business process performance in a circular economy. *Resources, Conservation and Recycling*, *152*, 104502.

Bisio, I., et al., 2018. Exploiting context-aware capabilities over the internet of things for industry 4.0 applications. IEEE Network 32 (3), 108–114.

Bodrow, W., 2017. Impact of Industry 4.0 in service oriented firm. Adv. Manuf. 5 (4), 394–400.

Dallasega, P., Woschank, M., Zsifkovits, H., Tippayawong, K., & Brown, C. A. (2020). Requirement analysis for the design of smart logistics in SMEs. In *Industry 4.0 for SMEs* (pp. 147-162). Palgrave Macmillan, Cham.

Dangelmaier, W., Fischer, M., Gausemeier, J., Grafe, M., Matysczok, C., & Mueck, B. (2005). Virtual and augmented reality support for discrete manufacturing system simulation. *Computers in Industry*, *56*(4), 371-383.

Fareri, S., Fantoni, G., Chiarello, F., Coli, E., & Binda, A. (2020). Estimating Industry 4.0 impact on job profiles and skills using text mining. *Computers in Industry, 118*. https://doi.org/10.1016/j.compind.2020.103222

Fern´andez-Miranda, S.S. et al., 2017. The challenge of integrating Industry 4.0 in the degree of Mechanical Engineering. Procedia Manuf., 13, pp.1229–1236. Available at: https://doi.org/10.1016/j.promfg.2017.09.039.

Geissbauer, R. et al., 2018. Global Digital Operations Study 2018. Digital Champions. How industry leaders build integrated operations ecosystems to deliver end-to-end customer solutions, Available at:
https://www.strategyand.pwc.com/industry4-0.

Glas, A.H., Kleemann, F.C., 2016. The Impact of Industry 4.0 on Procurement and Supply Management: A Conceptual and Qualitative Analysis. Int. J. Bus. Manage. Invent. 5 (6), 55–66.

Govindan, K., Kannan, D., Jørgensen, T. B., & Nielsen, T. S. (2022). Supply chain 4.0 performance measurement: A systematic literature review, framework development, and empirical evidence. *Transportation Research Part E: Logistics and Transportation Review*, *164*, 102725.

Haleem, A. *et al.* (2023) "Management 4.0: Concept, applications and advancements," *Sustainable Operations and Computers*, 4, pp. 10–21. Available at:
https://doi.org/10.1016/j.susoc.2022.10.002.

Hossain, M. S., & Muhammad, G. (2016). Cloud-assisted industrial internet of things (iiot)–enabled framework for health monitoring. *Computer Networks*, *101*, 192-202.

Javaid, M., Haleem, A., Singh, R. P., Suman, R., & Khan, S. (2022). A review of Blockchain Technology applications for financial services. *BenchCouncil Transactions on Benchmarks, Standards and Evaluations*, 100073.

Javaid, M., Khan, S., Haleem, A., & Rab, S. (2022). Adoption of modern technologies for implementing industry 4.0: an integrated MCDM approach. *Benchmarking: An International Journal*, (ahead-of-print).

Kalsoom, T., Ramzan, N., Ahmed, S., Ur-Rehman, M., 2020. Advances in Sensor Technologies in the Era of Smart Factory and Industry 4.0. Sensors 20 (23), 6783.

Khalil, R. A., Saeed, N., Babar, M. I., & Jan, T. (2020). Toward the internet of underwater things: Recent developments and future challenges. *IEEE Consumer Electronics Magazine*, *10*(6), 32-37.

Lerher, T., 2018. Warehousing 4.0 by using shuttlebased storage and retrieval systems. FME Trans. 46 (3), 381–385.

Li, Y., Dai, J., Cui, L., 2020. The impact of digital technologies on economic and environmental performance in the context of industry 4.0: A moderated mediation model. Int. J. Prod. Econ., 107777

Liu, Y., & Xu, X. (2017). Industry 4.0 and cloud manufacturing: A comparative analysis. *Journal of Manufacturing Science and Engineering, Transactions of the ASME, 139*(3).

https://doi.org/10.1115/1.4034667

Matt, D. T., Orzes, G., Rauch, E., & Dallasega, P. (2020). Urban production – A socially sustainable factory concept to overcome shortcomings of qualified workers in smart SMEs. *Computers and Industrial Engineering, 139*.
https://doi.org/10.1016/j

Novak-Marcincin, J., Barna, J., Janak, M., & Novakova-Marcincinova, L. (2013). Augmented reality aided manufacturing. *Procedia Computer Science*, *25*, 23-31.

Ranjan, J., Foropon, C., 2021. Big data analytics in building the competitive intelligence of organizations. Int. J. Inf. Manage. 56, 102231.

Rejeb, A., Keogh, J.G., Wamba, S.F., Treiblmaier, H., 2021. The potentials of augmented reality in supply chain management: A state-of-the-art review. Manage. Rev. Quart. 71 (4), 819–856.

Risius, M. and Spohrer, K. (2017), "A blockchain research framework: what we (don't) know, where we go from here, and how we will get there", Business & Information Systems Engineering, Vol. 59 No. 6, pp. 385-409.

Shukri, S.E., Al-Sayyed, R., Hudaib, A., Mirjalili, S., 2021. Enhanced multi-verse optimizer for task scheduling in cloud computing environments. Expert Syst. Appl. 168, 114230.

Sony, M., & Naik, S. (2020). Critical factors for the successful implementation of Industry 4.0: A review and future research direction. *Production Planning and Control, 31*(10), 799–815. https://doi.org/10.1080/09537287.2019.1691278

Sony, M., Antony, J., & Douglas, J. A. (2020). Essential ingredients for the implementation of Quality 4.0: A narrative review of literature and future directions for research. *TQM Journal, 32*(4), 779–793. https://doi.org/10.1108/TQM-12-2019- 0275

Strandhagen, J.W. et al., 2017. The fit of Industry 4.0 applications in manufacturing logistics: a multiple case study. Adv. Manuf. 5(4), pp.344–358. Available at: https://doi.org/10.1007/s40436-017-0200-y

Toka, A., 2013. Cloud Computing in Supply Chain Management: An Overview. E-Logistics and E-Supply Chain Management, (January), pp.218–231.

Zheng, M., Wu, K., 2017. Smart spare parts management systems in semiconductor manufacturing. *Ind. Manage. Data Syst.* 117 (4), 754–763.

Zhong, R.Y., et al., 2017. Intelligent Manufacturing in the Context of Industry 4.0: A Review. Engineering 3, 616–630.

Chapter 2
Green Technology Solutions: A way forward to achieving a Sustainable Industry 4.0

Jacinta Dsilva[1] Jasmina Locke[1]
[1]SEE Institute, Sustainable City, Dubai-UAE

Abstract: The fourth industrial revolution, Industry 4.0, and digital transformation have the potential to significantly enhance sustainability in every aspect of a business. The evolution of production and industrial process-related technologies such as the Internet of Things and green technologies (GT) are contributing to finding sustainability-enabled solutions. This revolution is reshaping lives and surroundings around humans, making them conscious of the changes that can provide a better future for the generations to come. GT has various advantages, particularly reduced energy consumption, remote maintenance, and efficient processing, and are already proving to be a path-breaking innovation leading toward achieving sustainability-related goals. This chapter begins with an overview of Industry 4.0 and the technologies involved, as well as how these technologies are contributing towards a sustainable future. The chapter further focuses on how green technologies can assist in achieving specific SDGs. The chapter concludes by providing impactful solutions to assist businesses in making strategic decisions leading toward sustainable Industry 4.0.

Keywords: Industry 4.0, Sustainability, Sustainable Development Goals, Green technologies, impactful solutions

1. Introduction

The first industrial revolution (IR) made remarkable changes to the planet. As a result, the urban population increased, and the standard of living improved noticeably, however, this expansion led to an exponential increase in the world population. Eventually, extreme developments caused a severe impact on the planet's environment and have been progressing at a much faster rate. Each industrial revolution improved systems, processes, and our lives, for example, Industry 3.0 saw the emergence of nuclear energy (Vries, 2008). During the early years of the 21st century, the world witnessed another transformation: the fourth IR Industry 4.0 (I4.0), fueled by digital transformation (Ardito et al., 2019). I4.0 encompassed flexible automation, cyber-physical systems, the Internet of Things, and several others. This revolution instantly received recognition since industries were struggling with producing using non-renewable resources. I4.0 garnered huge attention from the industry and governments due to the way it could contribute to environmental, economic, and social aspects, therefore, businesses must focus on sustainable development in line with the Triple Bottom Line (TBL) perspective which highlights the 3Ps: People, Planet and Profit (Singh et al., 2021).

The United Nations defined sustainability as *"meeting the needs of the present without compromising the ability of future generations to meet their own needs."* Hence, it aims at ensuring sustainable living for all in the present and for future generations, addressing issues such as climate change and environmental degradation. However, focusing on sustainability is a holistic approach and should be done organically with the active involvement of people to make sustainable choices. Therefore, it is important to understand the impacts of I4.0 on sustainability and how it can contribute to fighting some of the challenges of the century. I4.0 enhances green technologies (GT) in working towards achieving sustainable changes in societies and developing smarter future communities. GT is also known for enhancing profitability while reducing environmental degradation and conserving natural resources.

2.   Industry 4.0

The industry 4.0 (I4.0) concept was developed by the German government in 2011, declaring it a crucial strategy for industrial production. I4.0 initially was referred to smart and autonomous factories with machines and production units that could communicate with each other through intelligent technologies. These days, it involves the digital transformation of the industry and the consumer markets, which means that it has evolved from automation in manufacturing to digitizing the entire value delivery network (Schroeder et al., 2019). The Internet of Things (IoT) and the Internet of Services (IoS) are the basic technologies used in connecting industries internally and externally, while cyber-physical systems (CPS) are used throughout the operations of the supply chain network. A range of technologies are also associated with I4.0, such as big data, cloud computing, additive manufacturing (3D printing), as well as blockchain (Laskurain et al., 2021). This technological revolution aims to provide flexible, fast, and personalized production with profitable business models.

3.   Industry 4.0 Technologies

Physical and digital technologies are two categories of I4.0 technologies (Bai et al., 2020). Technologies such as additive manufacturing are examples of physical I4.0 technologics whereas digital technologies refer to modern information technologies such as cloud computing and blockchain. Through various emerging communication, information, and intelligent technologies, these technologies can support production flexibility, efficiency, and productivity; thus, supporting sustainability, as exemplified below.

An increase in efficiency can be seen in additive manufacturing known as 3D printing. It is the process of creating 3D objects directly from digital models by depositing and stacking layers of polymers, ceramics, or metals. By using additive manufacturing, the quality and durability of products tend to increase. The weight of the 3D-printed part, such as for the aeronautic industry, is reduced by 25%, resulting in a 20% reduction in fuel consumption and a 10% increase in horsepower. 3D printing is also involved in the prototyping and development of the new GT (Ghobadian et al., 2020).

A technology that resulted in major advancements is the Internet of Things (IoT). IoT technologies are the primary motivator for Industry 4.0 practices as they contribute to manufacturing excellence and digital transformation. By digitalizing manufacturing, industries are adopting IoT technologies to reduce downtime, improve quality, and predictive and preventive analysis. Additionally, industrial robots are being implemented, for they are digitally connected and are the core of the smart revolution (Lee et al., 2022). Artificial Intelligence (AI)-based technologies are gaining traction in various fields related to sustainability, and climate sciences such as AI-augmented environmental monitoring and smart urban planning. Environmental sustainability AI focuses on resource conservation and pollution management. Furthermore, increased AI applications may result in efficient use of land and seascapes, enhanced environmental monitoring capabilities, and improved supply chain transparency (Javaid et al., 2022).

Blockchain-based technology has been a valuable invention of I4.0 and it provides transparency and security to businesses and consumers (Schinckus, 2020) combining characteristics to eliminate corruption and inefficiencies supports streamlining the process. Blockchain technology has the potential to play a significant role in combating climate change by improving carbon emission and clean energy trading and increasing climate finance flows. In this context, blockchain technology could be a potential solution to establish this market's credibility, demonstrating the effectiveness of the green bond market by reducing carbon emissions for key stakeholders. As a result, blockchain could promote further development of this market and contribute to the climate change strategy.

I4.0 technologies have been improving quality, efficiency, and productivity while contributing towards sustainability. There are other types of I4.0 technologies having a positive impact on the climate, like cobotic systems, cybersecurity, drones, mobile technology, nanotechnology, big data and analytics, cloud computing, and global positioning systems.

4. Green Technologies and Sustainable Industry 4.0

Sustainability was first discussed in 1987 in the 'Brundtland Report,' led by Dr. Gro Harlem Brundtland, and in 2015, United Nations designed the Sustainable Development Goals (SDGs) and the Paris agreement 2030 to reduce carbon emissions. SDGs are a broad framework for developing and developed countries and contain support to design policies and develop strategies to mitigate the consequences of climate change. Industry 4.0 and digital transformation are already making a substantial positive impact even though in their infancy phase and from an ecological viewpoint, they can assist in reducing energy and resource consumption across the value chain network (Kamble et al., 2018). Green technology (GT) is environmentally friendly in its production, and supply chain and is proving to be extremely influential in achieving sustainability goals. The aim of developing GT is to control climate change, protect the natural environment, and reduce reliance on non-renewable resources. Industries are already transitioning toward GT due to its potential to reduce the usage of non-renewable resources. GT provides sustainable fuel sources, particularly to the energy sector. Solar, wind, and hydroelectric dams can be used instead of fossil fuels since they are less detrimental to the environment and generate less harmful byproducts. For solar photovoltaic technology, semiconductor modules convert sunlight into electricity; they can be utilized as a green agricultural energy source for pumping water, village street and house lighting, and pest management. In comparison with other sources, wind energy produces fewer air pollutants or greenhouse gases. Wind turbines with capacities ranging from 900 W to 50 kW are installed in many parts of the world and can be utilized off-grid for pumping and treating drinking water, irrigation, as well as supplementing larger power plants (Shafiei & Abadi, 2017). Hydropower plants, which are commonly used for rural electrification, play a crucial role in facilitating irrigation and value addition at agricultural sources. The energy sector has a direct effect on the other sectors due to its reliance on energy. In the waste management sector, it has been beneficial for waste transportation and recycling. For example, by incorporating intelligent systems into smart bins that can automatically perform the classification and sorting of different waste categories while effectively communicating with devices (Hin et al., 2021). The smart bin application system makes a significant contribution to waste management efficiency. The transportation sector is heavily reliant on fuel and is a major contributor to greenhouse gas (GHG) emissions. As a result, this industry contributes by manufacturing electric vehicles, hybrid, and plug-in hybrid electric vehicles. Hydrogen fuel cell vehicles generate electricity by mixing oxygen with compressed hydrogen to create a flow of electrons. Some vehicles contain high-performance air purifier filters that filter the surrounding microparticulate while driving; similar technology is being developed for the air purification sector.

Green nanotechnology is the application of nanoproducts to promote sustainability. The use of nanomaterials for purposes such as efficient solar cells, practical fuel cells, and environmentally friendly batteries is being researched. Energy conservation, water treatment, increased renewable sources, and manufacturing changes through reduced speeds are among the most advanced energy-related initiatives (Qamar et al., 2020). Green nanotechnology has mostly been seen in purifying polluted water or extracting salt from seawater. GT has many advantages, including reduced energy consumption and efficient processing. As with most technologies, there is a potential for continuous enhancement, and is heavily reliant on the continuous development of I4.0, making it more effective and cost-effective.

5. Use of Green Technologies in Achieving Sustainable Development Goals

In the previous discussion, we saw how green technology can contribute to reducing carbon emissions, this part focuses on focusing on specific SDGs and the application of GT.

a. SDG 6 – Clean Water and Sanitation

This SDG stresses the importance of access to safe drinking water and hygienic environments. The use of IoT and AI in freshwater filtration and wastewater treatment ensures good water quality while reducing energy consumption. This is achieved through networks of sensors installed throughout the filtration and treatment processes, which monitor conditions in real-time and adjust operations accordingly. Moreover, green nanotechnology offers potential in water treatment due to its unique properties of effectively eliminating contaminants without adversely impacting the environment (Qamar, et al., 2020).

b. SDG 7 – Affordable and Clean Energy

SDG 7 focuses on providing quality energy solutions while reducing costs. I4.0 gives attention to promoting the integration of renewables such as photovoltaics (PV), wind power and bioenergy. It advocates a system of decentralized microgrids consisting of "prosumers," which are both the producers and consumers of power (Hua, et al., 2022). Connecting the microgrids allows the producers to sell excess energy to the consumers within the same locality, allowing for grid flexibility and stability, meaning that the intermittent supply from renewables is resolved and utilized in an efficient manner. This concept of decentralized technologies is fundamentally dependent on the connectivity that IoT brings and allows real-time demand response. It also involves centralized building management systems (BMS) that monitor building operations.

c.   SDG 11 – Sustainable Cities and Communities

This SDG focuses on creating smarter, safer, and more efficient cities. This is achieved through the integration of sensors and IoT into city infrastructure. The availability of real-time information about public transport, traffic, and parking spaces encourages sustainable commuting and facilitates better journey planning. Communities are also able to manage their waste more efficiently by digitizing bin infrastructure (Fatimah et al., 2020). Access to real-time information and IoT play a major role in preventing and responding to disasters, paving the way for resilient cities.

6.   Impactful solutions for Sustainable Industry 4.0.

As corporations adopt I4.0 technologies, their operations undergo significant improvements. Technologies that can be applied in businesses vary depending on the priorities, such as troubleshooting problematic areas, improving performance to meet the demands, or improving levels of quality and consistency. This entails prioritizing the areas where digitalization would be most beneficial. One of the ways to practically adopt I4.0 technology for businesses is the use of sensors; organizations can select the type of data the sensors can collect, and by connecting sensors to IoT, the collected data is converted into intelligent information. The IoT guarantees the collection of big data from various machines and cloud technology and provides the storage capacity and computation power to process them. Business intelligence systems allow access to information and its analysis to optimize decision-making processes in terms of efficiency and productivity by managing huge data from big data environments. For companies aiming to improve performance organically, additive manufacturing can be used to enhance the efficiency and quality of the components produced. Moreover, autonomous robots can be used for heavy items on a production line, preventing human injury; they can also be used for continuous production. Thus, technology implementation and business performance are inextricably linked. IT advancements can significantly impact individual and organizational performance, such as transforming businesses, increasing competition, and fostering innovation and sustainability. Technological advancement is important in many sectors of the economy. As a result, better technological implementation plays a significant role in improving long-term business performance and in achieving SDGs. Organizations undergoing I4.0 transformation can focus not only on a solid technological foundation but also on incorporating innovative practices. Governments must play a significantly active role in contributing toward sustainable I4.0 by developing support policies that create a conducive environment for innovation and technological advancements. These policies can drive change and promote the upskilling of employees and technological supply chain development. The support system will reap benefits to everyone in the economy in a certain way by creating an inclusive, sustainable and engaged community and financially stable economies.

7. Conclusion

In conclusion, the chapter aimed to develop an insight into Industry 4.0 and the technologies involved. Green technologies and their contribution to achieving sustainability goals were discussed. The application of I4.0 technologies such as IoT, Robotics, AR, and VR seems to attract stakeholders and it will further increase due to the potential green tech and I4.0 have in solving sustainability-related challenges. It is highly recommended that industries focus on proactively applying the I4.0 and GT to utilize the benefits of increased efficiency and reduced cost. It might be challenging for some industries to apply these technologies in the short run; however, digitalization is playing an increasingly important role in achieving SDGs and all stakeholders will have to involve in it sooner. Finally, to achieve sustainable development, industry and policymakers should work together to resolve the challenges and design strategies to achieve concrete sustainability milestones.

References

Ardito, L., Petruzzelli, A.M., Panniello, U. & Garavelli, A.C. (2019). Towards Industry 4.0: Mapping digital technologies for supply chain management-marketing integration, *Business Process Management Journal*, Vol. 25 (2), pp. 323-346.

Bai, C., Dallasega, P., Orzes, G., & Sarkis, J. (2020). Industry 4.0 technologies assessment: A sustainability perspective. *International journal of production economics*, 229, 107776.

Ejsmont, K., Gladysz, B., Corti, D., Castaño, F., Mohammed, W.M. & Martinez Lastra, J.L. (2020). Towards 'Lean Industry 4.00–current trends and future perspectives. *Cogent Bus. Manag.* Vol. 7, 1781995.

Fatimah, Y. A., Govindan, K., Murniningsih, R., & Setiawan, A. (2020). Industry 4.0 based sustainable circular economy approach for a smart waste management system to achieve sustainable development goals: A case study of Indonesia. *Journal of Cleaner Production - Article 122263, 269.*

Ghobadian, A., Talavera, I., Bhattacharya, A., Kumar, V., Garza-Reyes, J. A., & O'regan, N. (2020). Examining legitimization of additive manufacturing in the interplay between innovation, lean manufacturing, and sustainability. *International Journal of Production Economics*, 219, 457-468.

Hin, L. C., Hameed, V. A., Vasudavan, H., & Rana, M. E. (2021). An Intelligent Smart Bin for Waste Management. *2021 IEEE Mysore Sub Section International Conference (MysuruCon).*

Hua, W., Chen, Y., Qadrdan, M., Jiang, J., Sun, H., & Wu, J. (2022). Applications of blockchain and artificial intelligence technologies for enabling prosumers in smart grids: A review. *Renewable and Sustainable Energy Review* 161 - Article 112308.

Javaid, M., Haleem, A., Singh, R. P., & Suman, R. (2022). Artificial intelligence applications for industry 4.0: A literature-based study. *Journal of Industrial Integration and Management*, 7(01), 83-111.

Laskurain-Iturbe, I., Arana-Landín, G., Landeta-Manzano, B., & Uriarte-Gallastegi, N. (2021). Exploring the influence of industry 4.0 technologies on the circular economy. *Journal of Cleaner Production*, 321, 128944.

Lee, C. C., Qin, S., & Li, Y. (2022). Does industrial robot application promote green technology innovation in the manufacturing industry? *Technological Forecasting and Social Change*, 183, 121893.

Qamar, M., Noor, M., Ali, W., & Qamar, M. (2020). Green Technology and its Implications Worldwide. *The Inquisitive Meridian,* 3(1).

Schroeder, P., Anggraeni, K., Weber, U. (2019). The Relevance of Circular Economy Practices to the Sustainable Development Goals. *Journal of Industrial Ecology* 23, 77–95.

Schinckus, C. (2020). The good, the bad and the ugly: An overview of the sustainability of blockchain technology. *Energy Research & Social Science*, 69, 101614.

Singh, S. Dsilva, J. & Kumar, R. S. (2021). Modeling the CSR Initiatives on Firm Performance: A Context of Emerging Economies. *Empirical Economics Letters,* 20 (3).

Shafiei, M., & Abadi, H. (2017). The Importance of Green Technologies and Energy Efficiency for Environmental Protection. *International Journal of Applied Environmental Sciences*, 12(5), 937-951.

Vries, Peer. (2008). The Industrial Revolution. Encyclopedia of the Modern World Volume 4, 158-161. (pp.158-161) Publisher: Oxford University Press 2008.Khan, S., Ali, S. and Singh, R. (2022). Determinants of Remanufacturing Adoption for Circular Economy: A Causal Relationship Evaluation Framework, *Applied System Innovation,* 5(4), 62. https://doi.org/10.3390/asi5040062.

Khan, S., Singh, R. and Kirti. (2021). Critical Factors for Blockchain Technology Implementation: A Supply Chain Perspective, *Journal of Industrial Integration and Management,* 2150011.
https://doi.org/10.1142/s2424862221500111.

Khan, S., Singh, R., Haleem, A., Dsilva, J. and Ali, S. (2022). Exploration of Critical Success Factors of Logistics 4.0: A DEMATEL Approach, *Logistics,* 6(1), 13.

https://doi.org/10.3390/logistics6010013.

Pachar, S., Singh, R. and Wahid, M. (2021). Implication of Renewable Energy in Sustainable Development in India: Future Strategy, *IOP Conference Series: Material Science and Engineering,* 1149(1), 012020. https://doi.org/10.1088/1757-899x/1149/1/012020.

Pachar, S., Singh, R.(2021). Role of Sustainable development goals and corporate social responsibility in India's growth: opportunities and challenges, *Empirical Economics Letters*, 20(2), 277-281.

Singh, R et al. (2022). Quality 4.0 in Healthcare: Application of the EFQM Excellence Mode. *Empirical Economics Letters,* 21(2), 1-19.

Singh, R. (2018). The Cause of Unemployment in Current Market Scenario, *Vivechan International Journal of Research,* 9(1), 86-81.

Singh, R., DSilva, J. and Kumar, R. S. (2021). Modelling the CSR Initiatives on Firm Performance: A Context of Emerging Economies, *Empirical Economic Letters,* 20 (3), 221-228.

Singh, R., Dsilva, J., Centobelli, P. and Tripathi, V. (2021). A review on Sustainable HRM: A study evaluating Sustainability for organisational development, The Empirical Economics Letters, 20(2), 1-10.

Singh, R., Khan, S. and Dsilva, J. (2022). A framework for assessment of critical factor for circular economy practice implementation, *Journal of Modelling in Management*, https://doi.org/10.1108/jm2-06-2021-0145.

Singh, S, Singh, R, Shandilya, T and Kumar, R.S. (2021). Digital security issues in emerging technology management, *Empirical Economics Letters,* 20(5), 205-213.

Chapter 3
Management 4.0 driven development of Optimization Tools and Techniques

Syed Mohd Muneeb

Institute of Business Management, GLA University

Abstract

The digitalization of industrial systems is referred to as the Fourth Industrial Revolution. Cyber-physical systems enable the vertical and horizontal integration of these production systems as well as the use of optimization tools to reap the rewards. In addition to identifying new research and development avenues motivated by new application options, this paper examines the effects of Industry 4.0 solutions on optimization problems and optimization methods. This study presented some of the optimization techniques and the ideas to incorporate them into different operations so as so attain the structure and goals of Management 4.0.

Keywords: Optimization model, industry 4.0, decision making

1. Introduction

Management 4.0 is a response to the market developments that have occurred recently, particularly in the 20th century as technology advanced tremendously and became important in a variety of occupations. Modern technology, integrated networks, cloud communication, and other platforms have revolutionized how businesses are handled. Management has also improved with the use of these tools. As a result, real-time data collection is ensured for better decision-making in response to new management demands.

In essence, Management 4.0 is based on two key tenets: technological industry transformation and customer behaviour monitoring. Along with making it possible for more original and inventive ways to generate income, the confluence of these ideas enables you to manage your organisation more strategically. Management 4.0 is a crucial part of Industry 4.0 which means the digital transformation of operations or production systems.

Management 4.0 is guided by some principles. These may be summarized as:

Customer centricity- This principal places customer at the center of all decisions from planning to product development to sales.

Channel diversification- Companies need to provide traditional platforms like the phone in addition to online and in-person support channels. All of this support must be omni-channel, or fully integrated, in order to be effective.

Automation- Companies can streamline operational processes with automated solutions and devote team expertise to strategic endeavors.

Data Analysis- Data serves as the cornerstone of management 4.0. You may select where and how to invest your resources and enhance business management with the help of accurate information.

Integration of sectors- The integration of many business sectors is another benefit of industry 4.0 technology, which makes it possible for everyone to work toward the same goals and tactics.

Industry 4.0 is transforming how businesses produce, enhance, and distribute their goods. The end-to-end digital supply chain, suppliers, and origins of the materials and components required for different types of smart manufacturing, as well as the end consumer, who serves as the final destination of all manufacturing and production regardless of the number of intermediary steps and players, are all crucial to understanding Industry 4.0. Industry 4.0 is thereby revolutionizing how various industries operate. Increased automation, preventative maintenance, self-optimization of process improvements, and, most importantly, a degree of efficiency and customer responsiveness never before imaginable are all results of digital technologies. enabling more direct forms of individualized production, servicing, and consumer/customer engagement (including gaining real-time and reducing the inefficiencies, irrelevance and charges of intermediaries in a virtual deliver chain model. This chain model works on the desires of Industry 4.0 on this customer-centric experience of an increasing number of disturbing clients who prioritize speed, cost efficiencies and price-delivered or value added modern services.

Companies can deploy digital solutions to achieve the goals of Management 4.0. Beyond the confines of a manufacturing facility, businesses can use digital solutions to address planning (and re planning) issues related to disruptions at suppliers or production facilities, operational issues with managing workplace health risks, and delivery issues raised by transportation modes or warehouses. These digital solutions can be employed at various operations to serve the needs of Management 4.0.

To be listed, these operations may include:

Planning the operations

Procurement

Inventory management and Warehousing

Transportation and Distribution

Production

Reverse Logistics

2. Planning the operations-

Planning, a crucial component of manufacturing and supply-chain operations, has historically been carried out in silos, with different teams managing demand forecasting, supply planning, production planning, logistics planning, and sales and operations planning (S&OP). Companies have been pushed to break through organizational divisions in order to increase end-to-end visibility due to disrupted global trade flows and value chains. As a result, it is easier to see how improved planning may have an influence. However, it also calls for increased analytical sophistication, cross-functional cooperation, and stakeholder involvement.

Think about demand projections. Traditional forecasting systems extrapolate past demand using relatively simple statistical procedures, with the underlying premise that the link between independent and dependent variables will probably not change. Independent variable may include past sales while future demand may come under dependent variables. In contrast, artificial intelligence and machine learning algorithms are used for autonomous planning. These algorithms use not only internal data, but also external datasets (uncertainties). These uncertainties may come from suppliers, buyers, weather forecasters, demographic criteria, and broader economic indicators. Incorporating these additional variables allows organizations to deal with varying dynamics and shocks from external sources. Advanced analytics can also optimise planning across the entire value chain in ways that traditional analytical tools could not. Moreover, these uncertainties can be modeled and solved using various optimization techniques such as fuzzy concepts, grey number concepts, etc to achieve Management 4.0 goals. Since products have so far been used in term of "smart products" to include information about customer's preferences and use responses, so as to spread the use of data. Smart products use automatized knowledge databases for the three main phases between product's design and development and manufacturing process- process planning, operation sequencing and scheduling (Tratenjak and Cosis (2017)).

Procurement-

Procurement's role goes far beyond the common misconception that its main function is to have goods and services so as to meet the internal needs of the organization. An efficient procurement process aims to optimize the entire process in order to increase efficiency and create significant business value. Procurement optimization provides numerous benefits and adds significant value to your organization as a whole. It increases efficiency in the procurement process, which has a knock-on effect of positive reactions throughout your organization. Optimization techniques integrated with technology can result in the procurement of maximum benefits. Tripathi and Gupta (2020) proposed a framework for the re-engineering of procurement process in industry 4.0. Optimization models embedded with the data obtained using modern technologies can help attaining Management 4.0 as the outcome of better selection of suppliers, timely ordering of raw materials, monitoring of stocks, checking the quality levels etc.

Inventory Management and Warehousing -

Inventory is critical in business because it is directly related to cash and cash flow. There are two forms of inventory- visible and invisible. Visible forms of inventory may have raw materials, work in process goods, and end goods. Non-visible forms may constitute bandwidth server and memory cards capacity. Thus, managing both forms of inventory is very crucial to remain in the competition. Inventory must be maintained in each stage in order to increase downstream stage satisfaction, cut costs, and guarantee the supply chain operates effectively and efficiently. Maintaining the least amount of inventory possible in order to fully satisfy downstream demand, or maintaining the proper balance between upstream supply and downstream demand, is known as inventory optimization. The core concepts of Industry 4.0 are digitalization, visibility, connectivity, and interoperability. Inventory management and optimization are changing as a result of the rapid development of Industry 4.0 technology (Yuan (2020)).

Transportation and Distribution

The traditional idea of logistics is undergoing significant modifications and alterations as a result of the fourth industrial revolution, a topic that has gained popularity. This is primarily due to the evolving market demands and the global market context exhibiting new key elements like flexibility aspect, pro-activeness, adaptability. These are praised by academics who lean toward the shift to Industry 4.0 and can be achieved with the incorporation of new intelligent technologies. Analyzing shippings, rates, and constraints for realistic load plans that reduce general freight spend and gain efficiency across whole transportation networks is a process know as transportation/ distribution optimization. This creates a practical, workable load plan for the shipment once real-world freight prices, permitted carriers, defined capacities, transit times, and other pertinent data are loaded into the optimization platform. Management 4.0 approach consists cyber-physical systems, Internet of Things, Cloud computing, Big-data sensors, Intelligent robotics etc that will help feed the data into the optimization models and algorithms to create efficient distribution and transportation plans. Technological advancements will help in creating optimized scheduling plans to satisfy the demand and supply constraints. The successful operation of a manufacturing system depends on the efficient and secure transportation of goods. Automated guided vehicles

(AGVs)have gradually replaced inflexible conveyor belts in transportation trends (Van Parys et al.(2018))..

Production

Manufacturing optimization is the process by which businesses look for ways to improve their production procedures. There are various levels at which a system or product can be optimised, varying from equipment improvement to waste reduction. This objective is achievable for the manufacturing sector with the development of Industry 4.0 technology. So, learning and using cutting-edge industry 4.0 technologies that are most appropriate for the process is the key to optimize a manufacturing process. The integration of various technologies into an autonomous, sensor- and knowledge-based, self-regulating manufacturing system is what industry 4.0 (i4.0) refers to (Dalmarco et al. (2019)).

The efficiency of the production process can be increased by using optimization techniques such as process mapping and design of future including process automation and cloud solutions, process improvement, lean six sigma using data analytics, product specific KPI, real time performance monitoring, optimized production schedules etc.

Reverse Logistics

The rise in popularity of the circular economy (CE) idea, which aims to keep products, parts, and materials in their highest usable and valuable state at all times, demonstrates how crucial it is for reverse logistics (RL) systems to operate effectively. Traditional RL, on the other hand, is unable to meet the demands of contemporary supply chains and must be improved through the use of Industry 4.0 technology. Reverse logistics include the back flow of the used or returned products which can be processed further to resold, reused, refurbished, repaired or re-manufactured, and waste which can undergo recycling or disposed. The opportunities and potential of Industry 4.0 for both the circular economy and logistics have rarely been investigated simultaneously, Birkel and Müller (2020). Space optimization is needed to dedicate an area for returns. Various optimization models can be constructed to work on various key performance indicators (KPI) of different operations. These KPI`s may include Return rate, cost per return or exchange, minimum fault rate, minimum cost of operations and minimum scrap rate. Mathematical models with the KPI`s as objective functions modelled as Multi-objective optimization problems can be proved worthy of attaining efficient solutions. Moreover, multi-criteria optimization can be used to assess the weights or importance of different KPI`s so as to have the prioritized solutions.

Optimization tasks and algorithms for Management 4.0

As discussed above, optimization techniques are very effective in the context of Management 4.0. They are useful in almost all the operations making them economical, sustainable and efficient thereby fulfilling the goals of Management 4.0.

Formalization of the optimization problems

An optimization problem is determined by its constraints and objective function. Finding the optimum method to do a task is a key component of many significant applied challenges. This frequently entails determining the maximum or minimum value of a function, such as the shortest distance to travel, the least amount of money needed to complete a task, the most power a device can produce, distributing products with the minimum cost, maintaining inventory with the least deterioration etc. These are also entitled as objectives of the problem. An inequality known as a constraint describes how the values of the variables used to solve a problem are constrained. Some examples of the constraints are office productivity software, local electricity supply, captive business process outsourcing unit, budget availability, manpower availability etc.

The standard mathematical form of an optimization problem can be represented as:

Minimize $f(x)$

Subject to $g_i(x) \leq 0$, $\quad\quad\quad\quad\quad\quad\quad i = 1,2,...,m$

$\quad\quad h_j(x) = 0$ $\quad\quad\quad\quad\quad\quad\quad j = 1,2,...,p$

Where $\quad g_i(x) \leq 0$ are called the inequality constraints

$\quad h_j(x) = 0$ are called the equality constraints.

$\quad m \geq 0,\ p \geq 0.$

The optimization problem described above is termed as unconstrained problem if it does not contain any constraint.

If the optimization problem has only linear constraint and a linear objective function, then it is called as linear programming problem. The name "Linear Programming," where the term "linear" refers to the linear relationship among the modelling variables, was proposed by Koopman T.C. in 1951. Due to linearity, a change in one variable results in a corresponding change in the other.

The standard form on an LP problem is given as

Maximize (or Minimize) $\quad Z = \sum_{j=1}^{m} c_j x_j$

Subject to

$\sum_{j=1}^{m} a_{ij} x_j \{\leq,=,\geq\}\, b_i,$ $\quad\quad\quad \forall\, i = 1,2,...,n;$

and $x_j \geq 0,$ $\quad\quad\quad\quad\quad\quad \forall j = 1,2,...,m.$

Where c_j, a_{ij} and b_i are all constants.

The class of nonlinear optimization problems (NLPs), where there exists a nonlinear functioned objective function and the constraints can have both linear and nonlinear functions, are the most challenging optimization tasks. The following are examples of nonlinear optimization issues relevant to Industry 4.0: Priority areas of this class of optimization include optimization of energy efficiency and topology. Both of these improve the efficiency of industrial operations. These operations include optimal control and predictive maintenance where a dynamic system is optimized over a horizon. The first major fundamental work in this field was named as Non-Linear programming given by Kuhn and Tucker (1951). Later, Rosen (1960) proposed the gradient projection method to solve NLP problems. Cutting plane method and Penalty function method were given by Kelly (1960) and Zangwill (1967) respectively.

The general mathematical structure of an NLP is given as

$$
\left.\begin{array}{ll}
\text{Maximize (or Minimize)} \quad Z = f(x) & \\
\text{Subject to} & \\
g_i(x) \; \{\leq, =, \geq\} \; b_i, & \forall i = 1,2,...,n; \\
\text{and } x_j \geq 0, & \forall j = 1,2,...,m.
\end{array}\right\}
$$

Where $f(x)$ and $g_i(x)$, $\forall i = 1,2,...,n$ are real valued function of (x).

Many real-world issues, such as the number of tanks and airplanes in an army, the number of physicians in a hospital, etc., require that the decision variables take non-fractional or integer values. Thus, an MP in which some or all of the variables are taken to be integers is known as integer programming (IP).

Concerning towards the real-life scenario of Management 4.0, it is recommended to be equipped with tools and techniques to deal with uncertainties in the parameters. The data of the parameters for the mathematical model and the relationship between variables and parameters are unknown or ambiguous. As a result, decision-making requires the use of uncertain mathematical programming without knowledge of all potential outcomes. Uncertainty is prevalent in a variety of industries, including planning and scheduling, engineering designs, supplier selections, transportation, logistics, supply chain management, disaster management, production, and finance. Researchers have developed MP under several types of uncertainties, including fuzzy, grey, probabilistic, interval, and uncertainty theory (Liu, 2007). These uncertainties are incorporated into the mathematical models to generate decision making patterns for Management 4.0.

Most real-world issues have numerous objectives that need to be optimised simultaneously. Furthermore, a problem's goals could be in contradiction with one another. In light of this, it is extremely challenging and uncommon to find a single solution that can maximize all of the objectives or goals. As a result, techniques for multi-objective problems produce acceptable answers rather than a single ideal solution. Management 4.0 decision making need to work upon several objectives for which mathematical models need to be structured under Multi-objective (MO) decision making scheme. There is an abundance of literature available for MO problems. MO is applied over almost every field where some of the recent works are due to Kamal et al. (2018), Muneeb et al. (2019), Muneeb et al. (2021) etc.

The general mathematical structure of a Multi-objective problem can be given as:

$$
\left.
\begin{aligned}
&\text{Maximize (or Minimize)} \quad Z = (f_1(\boldsymbol{x}), f_2(\boldsymbol{x}), ..., f_K(\boldsymbol{x})) \\
&\text{Subject to} \\
&g_i(\boldsymbol{x})\ \{\leq, =, \geq\}\ b_i, \qquad\qquad \forall i = 1,2,...,n; \\
&\text{and } x_j \geq 0, \qquad\qquad\qquad \forall j = 1,2,...,m.
\end{aligned}
\right\}
$$

The majority of problems in the actual world display decentralised decision making in general. MLP is widely utilised in a variety of industries, including transportation, supply chains, market economies, waste minimization, agriculture, urban planning, traffic planning, hospital administration, etc. These problems can be structured into mathematical models using the multi-level decision making scheme. The general mathematical structure of a decentralized decision-making problem with decision makers at different levels is formulated below. The model has m levels of decision making with total m decision variables. The leader is assumed to have control over first decision variable x_1 and the leader first solves his problem to start the solution procedure. The leader, then, passes the information of his solution to the followers at subsequent level. The followers in turn generate their solution after and in view of the solutions of the decision makers above their level. The process continued until the process terminates.

$$
\left.
\begin{aligned}
&\underset{x_1}{\text{Maximize}}\, F_1 = f_1(x_1, x_2, ..., x_m), \quad (I^{st}\ Level) \\[2ex]
&\underset{x_2}{\text{Maximize}}\, F_2 = f_2(x_1, x_2, ..., x_m), \quad (II^{nd}\ Level) \\[1ex]
&\qquad\qquad \vdots \\[1ex]
&\underset{x_m}{\text{Maximize}}\, F_p = f_2(x_1, x_2, ..., x_m), \quad (m^{th}\ Level) \\[1ex]
&\text{Subject to} \\
&G = \{(x_1, x_2, ..., x_m)\,|\, g(x_1, x_2, ..., x_m) \leq b\}, \\
&x_i \geq 0, \qquad\qquad\qquad\qquad i = 1,2,3...,m.
\end{aligned}
\right\}
$$

Early works in this filed are done by Candler and Townsley (1982), Bialas and Karwan (1984), Ben-Ayed and Blair (1990) and Bard (1991). Heuristics algorithm are used to generate solutions for multi-level problems by Gendreau *et al.* (1996), Yin (2000), Calvete *et al.* (2008), Hosseini and Kamalabadi (2013), Chaabani *et al.* (2018) etc. Some of the recent works in this field are due to Muneeb et al. (2018), Jalil et al. (2018), Adhami et al. (2017), Muneeb et al. (2019) and Muneeb et al (2019).

3. Future Research Perspectives

In the business world, especially for problems requiring immediate attention, the solution time is crucial. There are no known algorithms for NP problems that can produce their ideal solutions quickly. Fast heuristic procedures are required to arrive at a good but not always ideal solution. Heuristics should produce more straightforward models that exclude some less crucial aspects or heuristics-based techniques, such as genetic algorithms, ant colony algorithms, tabu searches, and artificial intelligence-based methods. One of the causes of real-time issues is system uncertainty brought on by unforeseen activities and occurrences, such as the breakdown of a machine that needs maintenance. Additionally, the environment in which the production system must operate is unstable and dynamic. Changes in consumer needs, product design, and processing technology are to blame for this characteristic. In many fields, managing these uncertainties is difficult. There are two key research axes in this field. In the first, the answer must be decided upon beforehand and cannot be changed once an unknown event has been realised. In the second, a plan is in place, and a re-optimization is necessary when an unpredictable occurrence occurs.

Regarding the future research perspective, the concept of multi-stage optimization is used frequently in Industry 4.0 as the results generated by the horizontal and vertical integration are very large and time consuming. Only the "important" decisions are made and the "less important" ones are relaxed in high-level stages, whereas "important" decisions are made at higher levels in lower-level stages. For instance, the four steps of production planning, scheduling, operating instructions, and process optimization are defined by the ISA-95 standard. In a stochastic, dynamically changing environment, rolling horizon decision-making is a useful option for making the best decisions. The decision-role maker's is to choose a course of action for a predetermined number of future periods in a way that ensures the best choices made for the first period will effectively support subsequent plans. Beginning with a replanning periodicity step, the second decision time period allows for the revision and updating of prior decisions.

Digital twins are frequently used as building blocks in cyber-physical systems. A digital twin's cyber component can do a variety of computations and simulations and, in addition, can give details regarding scheduling and optimization techniques. Since they can be used to support decisions based on simulations, predictions, and optimization before providing intelligent real-time control, knowledge-based digital twin solutions can also aid in production optimization.

A formal model called an ontology uses mathematical logic to define and define items as well as the relationships between them. They can be used in a digital setting because they can be characterised by mathematical models.

4. Discussions and Conclusions

Industry 4.0 requirements have been gathered and debated. While creating fresh Industry 4.0 solutions, these guidelines might serve as a guide. Each of these requirements affects optimization differently and can occasionally conflict with one another in real-world situations. To meet these demands, though, thoughts and solutions must be found. Examples that provide ideas for improvement were gathered. There are many optimization issues that need to be resolved in industrial settings, and frequently, applying sophisticated solution techniques is necessary. Management, planning, scheduling, and maintenance duties have all been recognised as significant Industry 4.0 emphasis concerns in this study. Due to their interdependencies, these tasks can all be characterised as complex optimization problems.

Given the inherent uncertainty in modelling, including a variety of objective functions and taking nonlinear interactions into account assist the design become more precise. The scale of the mathematical models that are put up, their complexity, the modularity of the problem, and the stability of the solutions are evidently important considerations based on the aforementioned aspects. All of these have a significant impact on the set optimization tasks' resolution, accuracy, and software-based administration. The fact that solving integer-value optimization tasks needs mathematical solvers to take an exponentially large number of steps serves as a good example of the difficulties in finding a solution. Finding the best solution is becoming more complex since, for instance, a scheduling task by itself formulates a challenging NP task that is frequently combined with other production and operational requirements. By breaking down models and using efficient modelling and heuristics, many of these challenges can be lessened. The ideal solution may be verified using formal methods and simulation tools, and by utilising digital twins, the precise role of efficiency improvement can also be shown.

References

Birkel, H., & Müller, J. M. (2021). Potentials of industry 4.0 for supply chain management within the triple bottom line of sustainability–A systematic literature review. Journal of Cleaner Production, 289, 125612.

Koopman, T. C. (1951): An analysis of production as an efficient combination of activities, in Koopman, T. C. (Ed.): *Activity Analysis of Production and Allocation*, Proceeding of a Conference, John Wiley and Sons Inc., London, 233-97.

Kuhn, H. W. and Tucker, A. W. (1951): Nonlinear programming, in (J. Neyman, ed.) *Proceedings of the Second Berkeley Symposium on Mathematical Statistics and Probability*.

Rosen, J. B. (1960): The gradient projection method for nonlinear programming. Part I. Linear constraints. *Journal of the Society for Industrial and Applied Mathematics*, **8(1)**, 181-217.

Kelley, J. E. (1960): The cutting plane method for solving convex programs. Journal of the society for Industrial and Applied Mathematics, **8(4)**, 703-712.

Zangwill, W. I. (1967). Non-linear programming via penalty functions. *Management science,* **13(5)**, 344-358.

Liu, B. (2007): Uncertainty theory (2nd ed.). Berlin: Springer Verlag 90i

Trstenjak, M., & Cosic, P. (2017). Process planning in Industry 4.0 environment. Procedia Manufacturing, 11, 1744-1750.

Tripathi, S., & Gupta, M. (2020). A framework for procurement process re-engineering in Industry 4.0. Business Process Management Journal.

Yuan, X. M. (2020). Impact of Industry 4.0 on inventory systems and optimization. In Industry 4.0-Impact on Intelligent Logistics and Manufacturing. Intechopen.

Van Parys, R., Verbandt, M., Kotzé, M., Coppens, P., Swevers, J., Bruyninckx, H., ... & Pipeleers, G. (2018, September). Distributed coordination, transportation & localisation in industry 4.0. In 2018 International Conference on Indoor Positioning and Indoor Navigation (IPIN) (pp. 1-8). IEEE.

Dalmarco, G., Ramalho, F. R., Barros, A. C., & Soares, A. L. (2019). Providing industry 4.0 technologies: The case of a production technology cluster. The journal of high technology management research, 30(2), 100355.

Gendreau, M., Marcotte, P. and Savard, G. (1996): A hybrid tabu-ascent algorithm for the linear bilevel programming problem. *Journal of Global Optimization*, **8(3)**, 217-233.

. Kamal, M., Jalil, S. A., Muneeb, S. M. and Ali, I. (2018): A Distance Based Method for Solving Multi-objective Optimization Problems. *Journal of Modern Applied Statistical Methods*, **17(1)**, 21.

Muneeb, S. M., Asim, Z. and Adhami, A. Y. (2019): A multi-criteria decision making model for the optimal planning of municipal solid waste under uncertainty. International Journal of Multicriteria Decision Making, 8(2), 105-132.

Muneeb, S. M., Nomani, M., Asim, Z., & Adhami, A. (2021). Assessing and optimizing decision-making policies of India with public employment growth as a key indicator toward sustainable development goals using multicriteria mathematical modeling. Journal of Public Affairs, e2635.

. Muneeb, S. M., Adhami, A. Y., Jalil, S. A., & Asim, Z. (2018). Decentralized bi-level decision planning model for municipal solid waste recycling and management with cost reliability under uncertain environment. Sustainable Production and Consumption, 16, 33-44.

Muneeb, S. M., Adhami, A. Y., Asim, Z., & Jalil, S. A. (2019). Bi-level decision making models for advertising allocation problem under fuzzy environment. International Journal of System Assurance Engineering and Management, 10(2), 160-172.

Muneeb, S. M., Nomani, M. A., Masmoudi, M., & Adhami, A. Y. (2019). A bi-level decision-making approach for the vendor selection problem with random supply and demand. Management Decision.

Adhami, A. Y., Muneeb, S. M., & Nomani, M. A. (2017). A multi-level decision making model for the supplier selection problem in a fuzzy situation. Operations Research and Decisions, 27(4), 5-26.

Jalil, S. A., Javaid, S., & Muneeb, S. M. (2018). A decentralized multi-level decision making model for solid transportation problem with uncertainty. International journal of system assurance engineering and management, 9(5), 1022-1033.

Chapter 4
The Impact of Industry 4.0 on Human Resource Management: Key Insights and Trends

Kamalesh Ravesangar

Department of Accounting and Business, Tunku Abdul Rahman University of Management and Technology, Malaysia

Rubee Singh

Institute of Business Management, GLA University, India

Hafinas Halid

School of Business and Social Sciences, Albukhary International University

Abstract

Digitalization across a range of industry and service sectors is transforming the workplace and human resources. The adoption of disruptive technologies associated with the Fourth Industrial Revolution or known as Industry 4.0 is reshaping the way people work, learn, lead, manage, recruit, and interact with each other. The aim of this book chapter is to contribute to the theoretical development of human resource management (HRM) in the context of Industry 4.0, promoting directions for the sector and the HRM professionals, organizations, and the workforce that are required to face the challenges of Industry 4.0. This book chapter promote insights on digital trends resulting from Industry 4.0 affect the field of human resource management, HRM Industrial Revolutions, interaction of digitalization in HR for the evolution of the digital age, competences needed in the Industrial Revolution in order to become more productive, human and digital.

Keywords: Industry 4.0; Human Resource Management; Digitalization; Technology

1.0 Introduction

In today's world, technology is crucial because it has a significant impact on every sector of the economy. Inclusion and implementation of technology in these sectors have both positive and negative consequences, but working conditions and methods are now more convenient and cost-effective. It is necessary to understand the concept of smart HR 4.0. The concept of HR 4.0 evolved from the German concept of Industry 4.0, which was a high-tech program launched by the German government to introduce digitalization into traditional industries (Roblek, Meko, & Krape, 2016). The primary goal of implementing this system was to direct and optimize the production system with minimal human intervention. The fourth technological revolution introduced the concept and technology of a cyber-physical system, the internet of things and the internet of services, a network of microcomputers, and so on. It also includes highly differentiated customized products, well-coordinated product and service combinations, and value -added services. As technology advances in the field of human resources, organisations can expect to make room for Artificial Intelligence and Data Analytics (Jain, 2014). It is obvious that as an increasing number of jobs become specialised, thus the knowledge required will become broader. Machine Learning can be used to improve enrolment and general representative administration programming solutions. There will be a need for simple, accessible, and well-designed tech solutions that aid in the resolution of HR issues despite time we live in. As a result, the implementation of technology may have a significant impact on labour and organisation in future, as well as changing the way operations are being carried out (Bonekamp and Sure, 2015).

2.0 What is Human Resource 4.0

Human Resource 4.0 is closely related to the concept of Industry 4.0 revolution in the field of human resources. HR becomes more automated in it, focusing its activities on strategic issues rather than manual, bureaucratic, and repetitive tasks. Thus, The Internet of Things, Big Data, and Artificial Intelligence are assisting in the automation of most HR processes which resulting in more efficient and lean teams. Through the application of technologies derived from Industry 4.0 (Sivathanu & Pillai, 2018) in the HR sector, a new concept was developed which making it more agile and ensuring worker welfare (Mazurchenko & Marskova, 2019) prior to entering the labour market and extracting human potential for new tasks. As a result, HRM 4.0 must now create a digital culture of digital people who are trained with digital tools, i.e., with the necessary skills to increase productivity. The new HRM 4.0 paradigms will have significant implications for training in competencies required for Workforce 4.0 and new job profiles (Ana et al., 2019). Future talents will necessitate the development of more strategic, coordinated, and creative activities, as opposed to fewer repetitive and easy activities which allow people to demonstrate their skills in more valuable activities (Becker & Stern, 2016; Fareri et al., 2020; Flores et al., 2020). As a result, tasks that were previously done manually and with individual analysis can now be automated and large amounts of data can be analysed quickly, intelligently, and precisely. Hirsch-Kreinsen and Dregger (2016) created one of the models proposed for Industry 4.0 and Socio-technical system (STS) change. Human resource management becomes the focal point of the human-technology interface relationship (Figure 1).

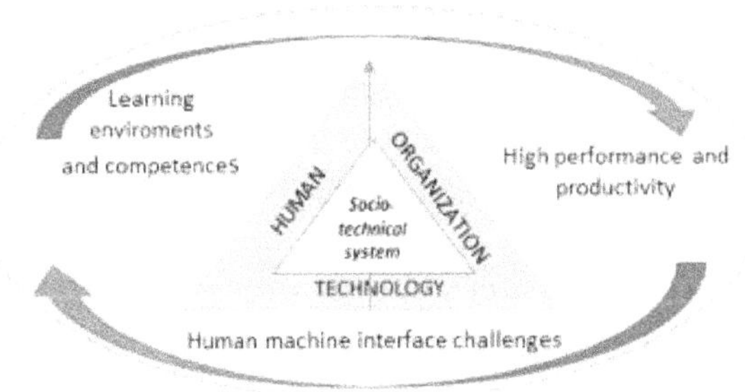

Figure 1 : *HRM 4.0 Background*
Source : Adapted from Dregger & Hirsch-Kreinsen (2016)

2.1 HRM Industrial Revolutions

The Fourth Industrial Revolution (4IR) is blending the physical, digital, and biological worlds which is blurring the lines between people and technology. The effects of these changes on how people work and businesses create value will be felt across all industries, economies, and societies, redefining the future of work. An initial response to this challenge is HR 4.0, a framework for shaping people strategies in the 4IR. Below explains Industrial Revolution to the Digital Transformation based on Figure 2.

2.1.1 The First Industrial Revolution

The initial industrialization period was followed by the first industrial revolution. It lasted from the late 18th century to the beginning of the 19th. The most significant changes occurred in industries as a result of mechanisation. Agriculture began to be replaced as the backbone of the societal economy by industry as a result of mechanisation. People were witnessing massive coal extraction at the time, as well as the significant invention of the steam engine, which created a new type of energy which fasten up the manufacturing of railroads that leads to rapid growth of the economy.

2.1.2 The Second Industrial Revolution

Almost a century after the first Industrial Revolution, the world is witnessing the second. It began at the end of the nineteenth century, with massive technological advancements in industries that aided in the development of a new source of energy—electricity, gas, and oil. This revolution resulted in the development of the internal combustion engine, which began to realise its full potential. Other significant aspects of the second industrial revolution included the growth of steel demand, chemical synthesis, and communication methods such as the telegraph and telephone. The inventions of the automobile and plane are regarded as the most significant (Rana & Sharma, 2019).

2.1.3 The Third Industrial Revolution

Another century has passed, and the Third Industrial Revolution has begun. In the second half of the twentieth century, the emergence of yet another previously untapped source of energy. The third industrial revolution saw the rise of electronics, telecommunications, and of course computers. Through new technologies, the third industrial revolution enabled space exploration, research, and biotechnology. In the industrial world, two major inventions, Programmable Logic Controllers (PLCs) and Robots have contributed to the emergence of an era of high-level automation.

2.1.4 The Fourth Industrial Revolution

Industry 4.0 refers to the digital transformation of manufacturing/production and related industries, as well as value creation processes. Industry 4.0 also known as the fourth industrial revolution, denotes a new stage in the organisation and control of the industrial value chain. Cyber-physical systems (e.g.,'smart machines') are the foundation of Industry

4.0. They use modern control systems, embedded software, and an Internet address to connect and be addressed through the Internet of Things (IoT).

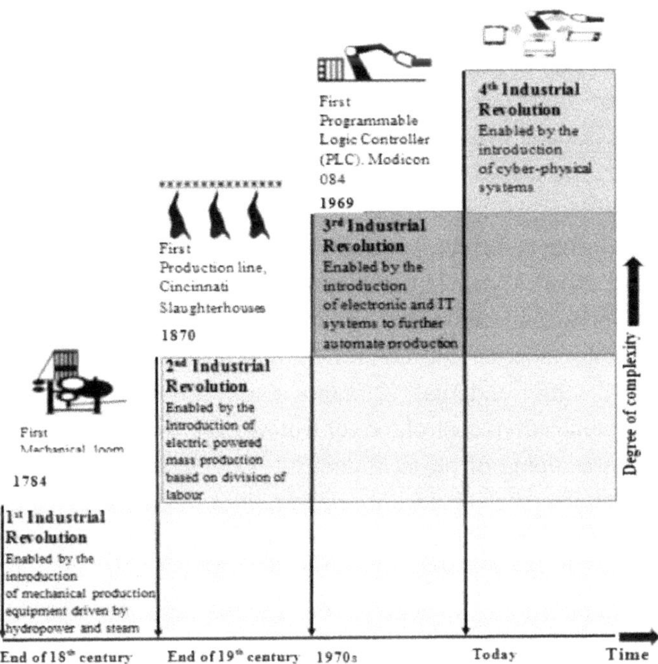

Figure 2 : *Definition of the various industrial revolution.*
Source : (Heng, 2014)

2.2 Components of Industry 4.0

There are three types of Industry 4.0 components such as technical components, social components, and production components. Technical components can be used to simplify work and life. In order to increase a country's competitiveness, social components focus on improving work quality and production components. Industry 4.0 is a recent technological advancement that includes the introduction of AI, IOT, 3D printing, cloud computing, CPS, and big data (Pandian, 2018). Cloud computing is a high-performance computing technology. Today's organisations are involved in complex decision-making activities that necessitate a large amount of data; these organisations required a diverse set of computing resources. Cloud computing assists organisations in overcoming such challenges. Organizations can now store data in cloud servers. All of these are supported by cloud computing and help organisations make complex decisions more easily (Xu et al., 2019). These are systems that control physical production using computers and other modern tools. CPS aids in intelligent monitoring and control such as Smart Factories (Bayraktar and Ataç, 2018). Cyber-physical systems typically combine sensor networks with embedded computing with feedback loops in order to monitor and control the physical environment that allow this external stimulus to self-activate either communication, control, or computing. The Internet of Things is the mapping of physical devices. The Internet of Things is expected to provide advanced capabilities of devices, systems, and services that exceed beyond machine-to-machine communications and cover a wide range of protocols, domains, and applications. Xu et al. (2019) It enables advanced services by connecting visible and implicit things that are supported by presented and evolving sensible data. It is a method for creating three distinct solid objects from a digital file. It is the process of designing layers of materials to create a 3D part. This is a subtractive manufacturing process alternative. Using the 3D process can be advantageous because it results in less material waste.

3.0 Drivers of Human Resources 4.0

Human resource management in organisations is required to perform various roles in the digital era in order to meet the needs that arise in that era. Human resource functions are expected to be more agile in responding to various demands of environmental changes, capable of managing complex data and information for making appropriate human resource decisions. The HR function must not only act as a strategic business partner in executing organisational strategies and bringing out the strategic work behaviour of organisational members through a set of HR policies/practices, but it must also be capable of utilising technology in carrying out its functions (Qadir & Agrawal, 2017).

Throughout the scope of this analysis, technology is more consistent with the assumed TPB (Theory of Planned Behavioral) behavioural regulation which is consumer resilience influenced by the available opportunities to maximise the ability of the proposed innovation (s). Regards of that, internal and foreign development tools (for example, ICT infrastructures, Web expertise, ICT engineering know-how, usage time, and developers) are considered. Although technical expertise extends beyond physical assets, it demands intangible capabilities that can create competitive advantages for innovators because abilities and know-how accompany physical assets and become more difficult to replicate rivals. Nonetheless, as the activities of digital networks expand beyond fundamental principles thus anonymity, protection, and security are critical concerns.

T-O-E is a classic concept that suggests a definitive set of variables that describe and forecast the likelihood of an innovation or technology being implemented (Pudjianto et al, 2011). According to the researchers, the system defines implementation in terms of a variety of internal and external innovations. Besides, the T-O-E as in Figure 3 postulates the analogy towards Actor-Network Theory (ANT) postulate, as it emphasises complex capacities and the reciprocal involvement of technological and social networks. Next, T-O-E is the only IS paradigm that focuses on social and behavioural constructivism, taking into account the interaction of technological progress and environmental circumstances (Al-Qirim et al., 2006).

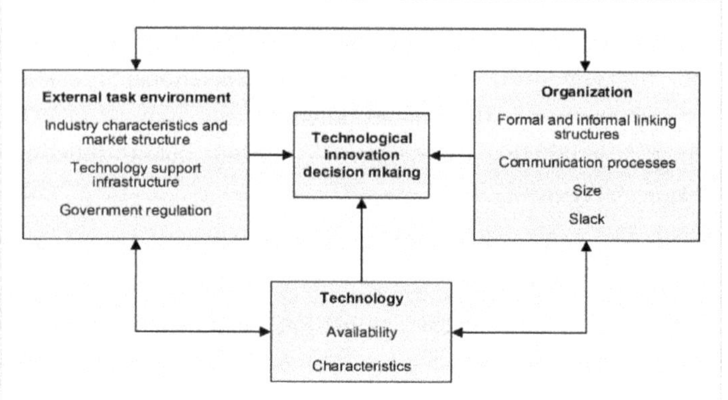

Figure 3 : *TOE adoption theoretical framework*
(Tornatzky et al., 1990)

4.0 Digital HRM

4.1 Digital Human Resource Management (HRM)

The evolution of digital human resource management is dependent on the continued development of information technology, which is a component of human resource management (HRM). All technologies are reappearing in new forms to attract and keep more personnel in the modern business sector. The most significant shift in HRM took place when traditional HRM was replaced with digital HRM. This shift came as a result of the implementation of new policies and strategies to attract organizations. Additionally, Saini (2018) defined digital HRM as the maintenance of all HRM works with the support of technology, via a variety of applications and the internet.

4.2 How digital HR works?

Schwab (2016), in the "Fourth Industrial Revolution," described how digital technologies have radically changed individual and societal life, working style, and how organisations operate their organisation and business. This includes how people live their lives, how they work, and how organisations do business. Therefore, for an organisation to remain competitive in this era, digitization is something that needs to be implemented, particularly in the area of human resource management. Traditional methods of recruitment and selection, for instance, are unable to simultaneously reach a large number of people across a wide geographic area.

Another illustration of this can be found in the realm of employee training and development. Employees can gain access to information regarding training programmes from remote locations, attend training in virtual classrooms, and evaluate their progress through a system or portal. Additionally, research conducted by Nawaz and Gomes (2017) found that HR information systems are beneficial to HR processes and also serve as a strategic tool for the development of organisations. This was reported in their findings. In addition, the technology is acting as an enabler for better performance through "cloud-based services, decision-enabling analytics, borderless teams, and real-time talent management across the organisation."

The second stage is known as "outward," and it involves either the employee or management level. This stage digitally enables both the employee and management levels. They plan to make use of mobile devices so that workers can carry out their duties in a manner that is more effective and productive (Saini, 2018). Employees will be better informed, more engaged, and more alert as a result of being able to handle and perform their tasks anywhere and at any time, which will ultimately result in real-time feedback being provided to management. The third is "across," which refers to changes made to the entirety of the organisation. The digitization of the organization's processes will result in new innovations, new collaborations, and new strategic approaches (Saini, 2018). The workers will become global workers as a result of the fact that they will share and bring their knowledge and ideas to a global level.

5.0 Digital Human Resource Management Practices

To gain a thorough understanding of what digital HRM is, it is necessary to define HRM. The finest HRM strategies, according to Amladi (2017), include "recruitment and selection, socialisation, job design, training and development, participation, career growth, performance appraisal, employee incentive, and job security." In addition, HRM can be defined as the management of human resources to facilitate the expansion of an organisation. The successful adoption and implementation of the Fourth Industrial Revolution by any organisation is contingent on that organization's ability to successfully apply ICTs in HRM operations (Industry 4.0). Nowadays, the majority of the duties and HR activities carried out by organisations have been automated. In today's interconnected world, businesses are looking for ways to acquire and keep a highly qualified workforce that are more time and cost efficient if they wish to continue to be competitive in the marketplace. Utilizing various forms of technology, most notably the internet, has proven to be a successful and widely adopted method for accomplishing this objective. The main purpose of the recruitment function is to identify, attract, and employ individuals who possess the highest levels of expertise. Having said that, the fact that there is a growing level of competition for talent in the market for jobs has made this task quite difficult. Companies are being required to broaden their search for applicants beyond local and domestic borders in order to find talent that is qualified. This trend is expected to continue. As a consequence of this, they have started recruiting potential employees via the internet in order to fill the available positions. Given that more than a million individuals search for job postings online, it is not surprising that firms of all sizes are resorting to online recruitment.

6.0 Future Scope

A future study should make some recommendations. First, by studying from a different angle, further research can determine the element of technology that Industrial Revolution 4.0 is focusing on for human resources. Many studies will be discovered in the future. This circumstance will make it easier for a prospective researcher to conduct new research. The future researcher should understand the research purpose as well as have a general understanding of the Industrial Revolution 4.0. Finally, a future study can be conducted to determine the impact of the Industrial Revolution 4.0 on human resources by focusing on a single issue. Future research should focus on social network theory to unravel the network linking human resource management and IR 4.0 knowledge (Shaharudin et al., 2019). It is critical for future research to determine how worker productivity can be measured. Productivity is important not only for some level of control, but also to optimise the process and increase motivation, both of which will have a positive impact in the near future and also in the company's distant future. Furthermore, the innovations on the company floor known as the primary source of development but also importance of employee motivation as well as management can be another very interesting and important future research area.

7.0 Conclusion

In nutshell, this chapter shows that in order for businesses to be able to deal with the transformational challenges of Industry 4.0, it must develop a successful Smart HR 4.0 strategy. New technologies such as Big Data and artificial intelligence will automate most human resource processes, resulting in more efficient and leaner HR teams. Intelligent mobile applications, as well as virtual and augmented reality, will attract the next generation of talent to businesses and enable them to interact across distances. Changes in organisational structures and leadership styles will be required for Smart HR 4.0 to be implemented effectively which allowing it to play a more strategic role in the company's overall growth. As a result, managers must adopt appropriate management approaches in order to survive and grow in the fourth Industrial Revolution. In this Industry 4.0 era, innovation is essential. People's capability is required for innovation which is aided by learning and knowledge.

References

Al-Qirim, N. (2006). The role of the government and e-commerce adoption in small businesses in New Zealand. *International Journal of Internet and Enterprise Management*, 4, 293–313.

Amladi, P. (2017). HR's guide to the digital transformation: ten digital economy use cases for transforming human resources in manufacturing. *Strategic HR Review, 16*(2), 66-70.

Ana, A., Meirawan, D., Kustiawan, I., Supriatna, N., Nugraha, E., Minghat, A. D., Muktiarni, & Dwiyanti, V. (2019). Future jobs in coming of industry revolution 4.0. *International Journal of Advanced Science and Technology*, 29(5), 567–574

Becker, T., & Stern, H. (2016). Future trends in human work area design for cyberphysical production systems. *Procedia CIRP*, 57, 404–409.

Bonekamp, L., & Sure, M. (2015). Consequences of Industry 4.0 on human labour and work organisation. *Journal of Business and Media Psychology*, 6(1), 33-40.

Das, S., & Sureshkrishna, G. Challenges of digitalisation for HR Professionals: An Exploratory Study. *International Journal Of Innovative Research In Technology*, 6 (1), 2019.

Dregger, J., Hirsch-Kreinsen (2016), "The digitization of manufacturing and its societal challenges: a framework for the future of industrial labor", *IEEE International Symposium on Ethics in Engineering, Science and Technology (ETHICS)*, 1-3

Fareri, S., Fantoni, G., Chiarello, F., Coli, E., & Binda, A. (2020). Estimating Industry 4.0 impact on job profiles and skills using text mining. *Computers in Industry*, 118. https://doi.org/10.1016/j.compind.2020.103222

Flores, E., Xu, X., & Lu, Y. (2020). Human Capital 4.0: A workforce competence typology for Industry 4.0. *Journal of Manufacturing Technology Management*, 31(4), 687–703.

Halid, H., Halim, S. N. A., & Ravesangar, K. (2022). Human Resource Management Practices in the Digital Era. In *Technological Challenges* (pp. 109-158). Springer, Cham.

Heng (2014). Industry 4.0: *Upgrading of Germany's Industrial Capabilities on the Horizon*. Academic Press.

Jain, S (2014). Virtual Factory Revisited for Manufacturing Data Analytics. *Proceedings of the 2014 Winter Simulation Conference*, pg 887- 898

Maršíková, K., & Mazurchenko, A. (2019). Digitalization: transforming the nature of HRM processes and HR professionals' competencies. *Proceedings of the 14th International Conference Liberec Economic Forum*, 291-301.

O. Bayraktar, C. Atac (2018). The effects of Industry 4.0 on Human resources management. *Researchgate*.

Pandian, M. S. S. (2018). Impact of fourth industrial revolution in human resource management. *International Journal for Research Trends and Innovation*. 3(2), 59-61

Parry, E., & Strohmeier, S. (2014). HRM in the digital age-digital changes and challenges of the HR profession. *Employee Relations*, 36(4).

Pfeffer, J (1994). Competitive advantage through people. *California Management Review*, 36, 9--28.

Pudjianto, B., Zo, H., Ciganek, A. P., & Rho, J. J. (2011). Determinants of e- government assimilation in Indonesia: An empirical investigation using a TOE framework. *Asia Pacific Journal of Information Systems,* 21(1), 49-80.

Qadir, A. and Agrawal, S. (2017). HR Transformation through Human Resource Information System: Review of Literature. *Journal of Strategic Human Resource Management*, 6(1),30.

Rana, G., & Sharma, R. (2019). Emerging human resource management practices in Industry 4.0. *Strategic HR Review*, 18(4), 176–181.

Rao, P., & Holt, D. (2005). Do green supply chains lead to competitiveness and economic performance?. *International journal of operations & production management*.

Roblek, V., Mesko, M., and Krapez, A. (2016). A complex view of industry 4.0. *International Journal of Production*, 6:1–11.

Saini S (2018). Digital HRM and its Effective Implementation: An Empirical Study. *International Journal of Management Studies*, 2(7).

Siddiquei, N. L., & Khalid, R. (2021). Development and validation of learning style scale for e-learners. *SAGE Open*, *11*(2), 21582440211022324.

Shaharudin, M. S., Fernando, Y., Jabbour, C. J. C., Sroufe, R., & Jasmi, M. F. A. (2019). Past, present, and future low carbon supply chain management: A content review using social network analysis. *Journal of cleaner production*, 218, 629-643.

Tornatzky, Louis G., Mitchell. Fleischer, and Alok K. Chakrabarti (1990). The Processes of Technological Innovation. Lexington, Mass: *Lexington Books*.

Xu, Wei (2019). Toward Human-Centered AI: *A Perspective from Human-Computer Interaction*, pp.

Khan, S., Ali, S. and Singh, R. (2022). Determinants of Remanufacturing Adoption for Circular Economy: A Causal Relationship Evaluation Framework, *Applied System Innovation,* 5(4), 62. https://doi.org/10.3390/asi5040062.

Khan, S., Singh, R. and Kirti. (2021). Critical Factors for Blockchain Technology Implementation: A Supply Chain Perspective, *Journal of Industrial Integration and Management,* 2150011.
https://doi.org/10.1142/s2424862221500111.

Khan, S., Singh, R., Haleem, A., Dsilva, J. and Ali, S. (2022). Exploration of Critical Success Factors of Logistics 4.0: A DEMATEL Approach, *Logistics,* 6(1), 13.

https://doi.org/10.3390/logistics6010013.
Pachar, S., Singh, R. and Wahid, M. (2021). Implication of Renewable Energy in Sustainable Development in India: Future Strategy, *IOP Conference Series: Material Science and Engineering,* 1149(1), 012020. https://doi.org/10.1088/1757-899x/1149/1/012020.

Pachar, S., Singh, R.(2021). Role of Sustainable development goals and corporate social responsibility in India's growth: opportunities and challenges, *Empirical Economics Letters*, 20(2), 277-281.

Singh, R et al. (2022). Quality 4.0 in Healthcare: Application of the EFQM Excellence Mode. *Empirical Economics Letters,* 21(2), 1-19.

Singh, R. (2018). The Cause of Unemployment in Current Market Scenario, *Vivechan International Journal of Research,* 9(1), 86-81.

Singh, R., DSilva, J. and Kumar, R. S. (2021). Modelling the CSR Initiatives on Firm Performance: A Context of Emerging Economies, *Empirical Economic Letters,* 20 (3), 221-228.

Singh, R., Dsilva, J., Centobelli, P. and Tripathi, V. (2021). A review on Sustainable HRM: A study evaluating Sustainability for organisational development, The Empirical Economics Letters, 20(2), 1-10.

Singh, R., Khan, S. and Dsilva, J. (2022). A framework for assessment of critical factor for circular economy practice implementation, *Journal of Modelling in Management,* https://doi.org/10.1108/jm2-06-2021-0145.

Singh, S, Singh, R, Shandilya, T and Kumar, R.S. (2021). Digital security issues in emerging technology management, *Empirical Economics Letters,* 20(5), 205-213.

Chapter 5
Management in the age of Artificial Intelligence

Manish Kumar Sharma

Department of Humanities and Social Sciences

Indian Institute of Technology, Kharagpur

Abstract

The global economic scenario is changing very fast just in a short time period of two to four years, as we have seen in the last couple of years in terms of trade wars between the US and China, Shocks like the Covid-19 pandemic, and Russia-Ukraine war and now further the expectation of a global recession. Managers of the new age need to be super sensitive to these fast-paced economic changes happening around the business environment and have to gauge in advance how these are going to impact their business. Keeping this in mind managers need to upskill themselves. There is a revolution due to technology in every field. Parts of human tasks are becoming automated and now the main task of humans, that is thinking and decision making is going to be augmented and, in some cases, replaced by Artificial intelligence, making the technology much more powerful and efficient than previously thought of. In this chapter, we underline the current developments and possible future possibilities of Artificial intelligence and the preparedness a 21st-century Management has to be ready with, in the current era of rapidly evolving technology.

Keywords: Artificial Intelligence, Change, Future, Management, Technology

1. Introduction

The wave of Artificial intelligence is at its peak, more than its use there is more discussion about the possibilities and capabilities it can offer in different fields and areas of its application. But it is natural, as Amara's law says "there is overestimate of any technology at its starting point in the short run and underestimate in the long run". We will first know what AI is and its scope and then its impact on management, and its different components. Further, we will step by step explain how AI is going to affect and can change management and put some examples and use cases, what are future expectations, and what managers in that area need to know and understand to stay ahead and this technology for the betterment of their organization in every aspect.

The chapter is a go-to read for all the managers looking to understand AI and future managers who are afraid of AI being represented as a replacement for their jobs.

2. AI: Definition, and Scope

A manager needs to understand well what is AI and where it derives its power from.

Definition: The Future of Artificial Intelligence Act of 2017 defines AI as "any artificial system that performs tasks under varying and unpredictable circumstances, without significant human oversight, or that can learn from their experience and improve their performance. They may solve tasks requiring human-like perception, cognition, planning, learning, communication, or physical action (Hassett, 2019)."

The latest developments in AI have been possible due to the combined share of developments in computer hardware and Information technology. We can divide the development which backed AI into the below sectors -

- Core Hardware – Computers and exponentially increasing computing power

- IT and IoT – Internet, Internet of Things (devices), Cloud infrastructure, online computing

- Software – Core hand designed programmes to Intelligent machines

Computational capacity and data power the AI besides the human minds working on it.

The unprecedented internet connectivity has made the data to explode today and it is available everywhere like never before. It has complemented the surge in computing power, allowing researchers to test and develop AI algorithms on larger data sets. All data is moving towards digitization which has resulted in the emergence of big data (Brynjolfsson & McAfee, 2014).

In addition to these now you don't require to have a powerful computer personally, instead, you can hire one Amazon Web services, Microsoft Azure, and Google Collaboratory are extensively providing cloud computing services for use of the AI community specifically.

AI has recently caused remarkable changes in many disciplines viz. Engineering, Social sciences and research. The use of such disruptive technologies would also have a remarkable impact on economic theories. Seeing the history of the development of in technology, we can say, the bounds of rationality are going to become shorter for machines than humans.

Machines are now part of everyday decision-making (computers, mobile phones, IoT). Simultaneously they are heading towards becoming more intelligent with the help of Artificial Intelligence (AI). Alan Turing theorized that a machine is artificially intelligent if and only if we interact with them and we cannot tell we are interacting with a human or machine, called Turing test (Marwala & Hurwitz, 2017).

3. Why Is it important to study the Impact of AI?

People often give arguments that AI is overhyped and raise the questions whether it is right time to emphasize the focus on studying different aspects of AI. But the developments in this field are fast and changing and impacting the global scenario, let us see some examples below

• The IBM supercomputer that won to the world champion Garry Kasparov in 1997, AlphaZero trained itself to play like a human (Hamdan et al., 2021).

• Economists find significant returns on student outcomes from AI "edtech" programs (Escuenta et al., 2017).

What separates AI from the rest of the Automation technologies is its highly complex human-like decision logic, instead of automating a specific process or repetitive labour tasks.

Google, Amazon, Microsoft, Tesla, Softbank, Mitsubishi, General Motors and many big companies are investing heavily in AI today. For example, the dream of a driverless car once thought to be difficult has become a commercial possibility today because of the advent of Artificial Intelligence. Similarly, a large no. of scientists in possibly all areas of science are exploring the use of AI.

Theories of the past will have to change and adapt in light of Artificial intelligence. We propose to study this recent advancement of technology from an organizational and management point of view based on recent developments in AI.

Reasons to study AI's impact on Management – Managers have the power to direct, guide, and bring out the potential of AI if they use their authority properly and have a good understanding of AI and its impact in their departments and respective roles. There have been a limited number of studies on this subject, but most of them focus on the possible impact and do not clearly state the way forward for managers and they only give an overall view of the impact of AI but not according to different department-wise roles of managers in an organization. This chapter fills that gap by clearly specifying the changes and developments due to AI for different departments in an organization and their managers and what they need to do keeping in mind the future prospects and economy-wide impacts of AI.

4.   AI and its impact on an organization

We start by comparing the role of computers in organizations, and the change they brought. The production process has moved from completely mechanical and human-based to digital and computer-assisted production, which provides easy communication, better management of data, and fast and easy computation by the use of different software. With the help of computers and available digital devices, now an organization is able to generate huge data compared to earlier time periods. This data can be used to process and get insights from AI models.

For example, the quality department in an industry notes the standard quality parameters and checks the samples of output produced against defined standards. These readings are taken several times a day according to no. of batches and quantity produced. This daily data creates a huge amount of monthly or yearly data and if fed into an AI model can give process and quality improvement insights when matched with production input data and the efficiency of production can be highly improved.

We can soon see an AI management software, which takes its own decisions which are redundant and of low value. It may be called digital management or management 4.0. We may see multiple digital management platforms or AI robots installed in an organization that performs redundant management tasks and thus relationship and interaction between workers and management may change altogether. It may be seen as positive because the pressure and hierarchical stress will be reduced in lower-level workers as there would be a less human element in the management, while it may be seen as a negative development as it would lack the emotion and compassion a human being can bring along with his/her role.

Imagine as a top-level manager, you have to read a lot of reports, daily changing economic activities around the country and the world, and take important decisions accordingly. This task can be reduced to a simple task just by feeding the large data into an AI model and it would give summarized most important insights to the manager and thus would save time and increase his efficiency in taking decisions with more confidence.

AI can lead to changes in organizational behaviour, as the type of interaction between organizational elements will change due to automation and use of AI and new possibilities of synergy and conflicts may arise.

On a positive note, one difference between horses of the 19th century and today's manpower is that horses couldn't upskill but humans can, which can be a huge reassuring point to the ones fearing their job replacement due to AI. Likewise, today almost all of the tasks involve computers, in the future, the same will happen with AI. It will penetrate every task being performed in a business. If computers help humans work faster, it gives them more time to utilize it somewhere else and along with making them richer. As shown in Figure 1, Natural Language Processing (NLP) in AI performs semantic analysis, language translation, text generation and text summarization tasks, while in computer vision image/object identification, video activity detection, and video subtitle generation are done. Machine learning focuses on simpler models of AI to predict, classify and for regression, while deep learning uses complex and big models along with large data.

These all tasks under AI will impact every part of an organization whether at the individual level or process/system level. Deducing from these possibilities, an augmenting effect of AI can be idealized but cannot necessarily be generalized. There may be an increase in inequality as most AI resources would be available with big and powerful organizations, which will take and are already taking AI's first mover advantage. Interaction of managers in the future is going to be highly digital and AI-based, which means they would be talking to computers and instructing them to do tasks in place of manually doing tasks on their own, which can be seen at lower levels what voice assistance technology like Alexa is doing nowadays.

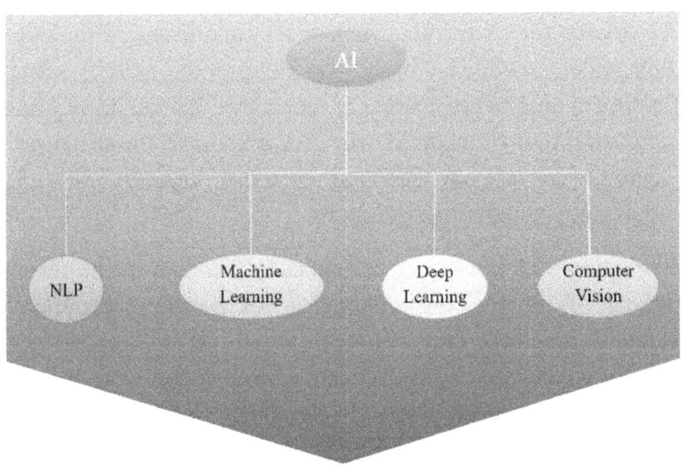

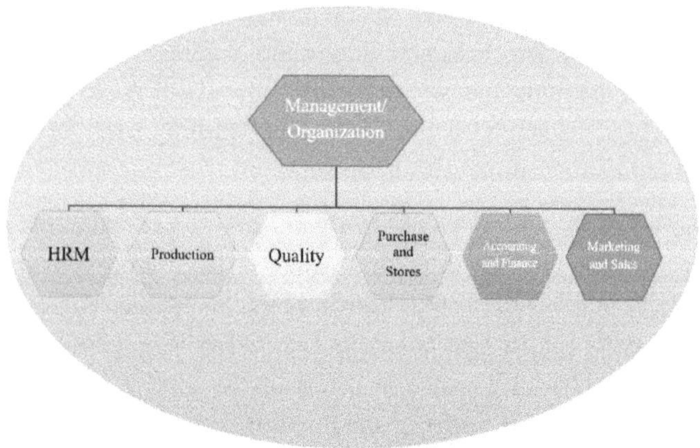

Figure 1: Impact of AI on different parts of
Management/Organization
Source: Author's Representation

5.   Examples and use cases

Many companies use video analytics of potential candidates for hiring predictions, while others use automated resume analytics AI tools for screening potential candidates, Employee engagement analysis based on employee activity data. Sentiment analysis of a video or report by a federal agency and summarizing it through AI will give a boost to the managers. Chatbots are already assisting customer care by handling redundant and repetitive questions.

Marketing and sales have dramatically changed in the recent decade. With the big emergence of online e-commerce companies and the high impact of social media, sales history, browsing history and other social media attributes have become an important part of expected sales predictions and similarly personalized targeted automated marketing is being done on social media platforms using AI. It has increased the reach of companies to a number of people as well as increased sales.

So, those who take the right decisions at right time well before their competitors by using AI will have an edge over other which don't use AI.

Most of the individuals are already interacting with AI in one or other forms like face detection and tagging on social media, image transformation, Virtual assistants which perform tasks based on audio commands, E-commerce, and chatbots. This will be the case for businesses as well. Most of the businesses will use AI in one or another form in the near future.

AI has also been used in Research and Development, like the development of new chemicals, discovering new elements or molecules, the combination of elements, studying the interaction of different chemicals, and discovering new drugs. In physics, a huge amount of data from the Large Hadron collider is analyzed using AI, and the data obtained for the discovery of the Blackhole for the first time was done using AI. Similarly, civil, mechanical and computer graphical designs are being done using AI, to give unimaginable and complex best design structures and use them in practical life applications. The supply chain and inventory management can also be automated and managed efficiently using AI, giving more time to humans to manage more complex tasks.

Recent AI-powered virtual news male Anchor Qiu Hao in 2018 & female anchor Xin Xiaomeng in 2019, have shown that this technology has passed the famous Turing test efficiently, and can work 24 Hours a day. These anchors delivered 3400 News reports and 10,000 minutes of screen time. This sets alarm for academicians to study the potential impact of AI in Advance, and bring out the different aspects of this new development in technology.

All the above examples show, the capabilities of this technology and some call it even the fourth industrial revolution in this information age.

6. What Managers need to keep in Mind, Recommendations for Managers

The managers of the present and future will definitely have to deal with AI at some or other stage of their work and therefore the first and foremost important task for them is to upskill themselves with the knowledge and working of AI. With that, they can understand what is the capability of this technology and thus can utilize it well for example changes in hiring practices, and changes in marketing and selling. Managers have decision-making power and therefore are key to unleashing the real potential of AI. For the same reason managers who have AI skills are expected to get the highest premium for having these skills. Training and development of manpower has also to be dealt with keeping in mind the applicability of AI in a particular department and need for the manpower. AI of today can write that is, can generate text, AI can take routine decisions, AI can predict better using large data, AI can design better, it can innovate better, it augments human capabilities similar to what computers did earlier and are still doing irrespective of the initial fear of computer impacting and replacing jobs.

Managers should try to avoid the monopoly of big firms over the power of AI and should advocate the need for the right regulations for AI uses. In some cases, AI may also have biases and needs to be dealt with care, according to the sensitivity of its application which otherwise can result in the wrong and costly decisions. For example, a biased hiring algorithm can cost the right person his deserving job while a wrong diagnosis of cancer may lead to the life of a human. However, AI may help in removing personal human bias in the recruitment and selection process but it may tend to select a similar type of profiles more and thus may hinder diversity. Sometimes investments in AI for businesses can be confusing initially, therefore managers need to define exact quantifiable metrics to measure the value added in terms of money, manpower, time and resources saved, efficiency improvement and increase in profit/sales.

7. Conclusion

We have delved into the importance of a well-developed understanding about Artificial Intelligence for managers. Many examples showcase the increasing scope of AI and it's not an exaggeration to call it as next General-Purpose Technology (GPT) just like Fire, Wheel, electricity, computers and the internet have been previously. Besides understanding what AI is, managers also need to use it efficiently as they are key decision-makers and thus have to make well-informed and conscious decisions so that they can make their organization future ready and ahead of the competition. They should also be conscious about the biases, ambiguities and uncertainties which come with AI and should try to quantify the value additions they are going to get out of it.

References

Agrawal, A., Gans, J., & Goldfarb, A. (2019). Artificial Intelligence, Economics, and Industrial Organization. *The Economics of Artificial Intelligence, June*, 399–422.

Brynjolfsson, E., & McAfee, A. (2014). The Second Machine Age: Work, Progress, and Prosperity in a Time of Brilliant Technologies. W. W. Norton & Company.

Byrne, D. M., Corrado, C. A., & Sichel, D. E. (2018). The Rise of Cloud Computing: Minding Your P's, Q's and K's. *National Bureau of Economic Research Working Paper Series, No. 25188.*

Escuenta, M., Quan, V., Nickow, A. J., & Oreopoulos, P. (2017). Education Technology: An Evidence-Based Review. 1–102.

Gertler, M., & Bernanke, B. S. (2014). Should Central Banks respond to movements in Asset Prices? *The American Economic Review, 91*(2), 253–257. https://doi.org/10.1257/aer.91.2.253

Hamdan, A., Hassanien, A. E., Khamis, R., Alareeni, B., Razzaque, A., & Awwad, B. (2021). Applications of Artificial Intelligence in Business, Education and Healthcare. https://doi.org/10.1007/978-3-030-72080-3_27

Hassett, K. A. (2019). The Economic Report of the President Together with The Annual Report of the Council of Economic Advisers. In *The White House* (Vol. 17, Issue 2). https://doi.org/10.1080/05775132.1974.11470048

Kahyaoğlu, S. B. (2021). The Impact of Artificial Intelligence on Governance, Economics and Finance: Vol. I. https://link.springer.com/10.1007/978-981-33-6811-8

Marwala, T., & Hurwitz, E. (2017). Artificial intelligence and economic theory: skynet in the market. In *Advanced Information and Knowledge Processing*. http://link.springer.com/10.1007/978-3-319-66104-9

Nilsson, N. J. (2009). The Quest for Artificial Intelligence. In *The Quest for Artificial Intelligence*. https://doi.org/10.1017/cbo9780511819346

Simon, H. A. . (1991). Bounded Rationality and Organizational Learning. *2*(1), 125–134.

World Economic Forum. (2018). The Future of Jobs Report 2018. In *World Economic Forum* (Vol. 31, Issue 2).

Chapter 6
Policy and Practice of Delivering Government Services through Technology

Kalpana Gopalan IAS

Additional Chief Secretary, Government of Karnataka, India

Leveraging technology for effective program delivery poses unique challenges. Technology is a tool that requires a capable state to be effective; also, it creates new power asymmetries. Across successive governments, India has emerged as a pioneer in building digital tools to improve program governance at the state and national levels. Has all this technology helped? Robust evidence is mixed and limited. Leveraging technology platforms for effective program delivery poses unique challenges. For citizens, the use of new tech-savvy tools can be alienating and intimidating. Using technology requires learning new ways to make demands and withdraw benefits, and new norms and modes of local behaviour. Tech-optimists suggest that problems faced by local governments and citizens in using technology, which manifest in reports of delays and exclusion due to poor infrastructure and connectivity are teething pains — side-effects of the transition to digital ways of interacting with government. Others see dark days ahead, where technology takes over governance, and the digitally illiterate, whether due to poverty, age or exclusion, are entirely left behind. My own view, born of years of experience and observation, is that technology opens amazing possibilities for reach and spread, but nevertheless needs to be implemented with caution to ensure inclusion and nuance.

In addressing the topic of public service delivery through technology, I therefore propose the following agenda:

We will begin with the objective of technology applications in governance, and the mechanisms by which e-governance works. We will then move to the three forms of e-governance, namely e-administration, e-services and e-participation, which I illustrate with examples. A discussion follows on state-driven initiatives, private sector initiatives and the recent trend of moving towards mobile governance. E-governance throws up its own set of questions and challenges, which I will discuss before finally giving some pointers which should underpin an e-governance policy for India. E-governance efforts have the two broad objectives: To strengthen government capacity and to empower citizens. It does this in 3 ways: easing public service delivery, enhancing accountability and promoting public participation.

We may identify three main forms of e-governance: e-administration, e-services, e-participation

- E-administration: improving back-end government processes through ICT-based systems of optimization.

- E-services: use of ICTs to improve provision of public services, be it universal or targeted to poor and vulnerable groups.

- E-participation: enables feedback from citizens to governing entities, allowing new forms of governance from below.

E-administration is a descriptor of government initiatives that are intended to improve its own internal functioning. E-tendering or e-procurement is a significant effort to streamline public procurement processes and is mandatory in Karnataka. As a unified platform for all government departments, E-procurement handles end-to-end procurement process in an online environment. Initiated in 2003 by a Karnataka Cabinet decision, it now has over 20000 users, 283 government departments and organizations, over 67000 vendors and 35 foreign bidders. E-procurement has handled over 3.3 lakh tenders valued at ₹ 3.5 lakh crores. As it holds several advantages for procurers and bidders, it has gained acceptability. It is also considered an important initiative to reduce corruption, avoid delay and improve administrative efficiency. E-procurement enhances transparency and accountability of government procurement processes, promotes competitive market-driven bidding, enables ease of access to the contractor community, provides a common environment for all types of tenders, and creates infrastructure for effective implementation of procurement policies. It involves less paper and thereby adopts green working.

Let us now move to e-services, which has found important applications in Karnataka's Public Distribution System. The ahara.nic.in portal is a transparent and open database of the PDS system which services over a crore of below priority line beneficiaries from priority households. Further, SMS messages are effectively harnessed for user convenience and information dissemination. Almost all information such as ration card status, ration card allotment and ration shop allotment can be obtained through SMS. Since August 2015, every ration card holder receives a monthly message which provides her PDS allotment for the month, as well as the amount she is required to pay. This micro-initiative has addressed the twin problems of under supply an over pricing simultaneously.

Speaking of e-participation, India's most comprehensive effort has been the mygov. portal, which enables the citizenry to directly connect with the Government, get recognized on a national platform, express views on matters of national interest, collaborate on key areas of development and governance, contribute to nation building by posting views on discussions and share ideas and viewpoints with others. Let us now move from specific initiatives to take a bird's eye view of the Indian e-firmament. Here we can see 3 broad trends: one, the critical role of the government in creating a conducive ecosystem for e-governance, two, the platform this has created for the emergence of micro targeted innovations in the private startup sector, and three the move from electronic to a more citizen friendly mobile governance.

The state's main role, in my view, is not so much to be a player in the e-gov space as an enabler. Some initiatives in Karnataka that have created this enabling climate are: Innovative Karnataka which has pegged Karnataka among the world's top 10 start-up destinations. E-Sugam, the Simple Uploading of Goods Arrival and Movement, in which 30 lakh forms per month are generated, has enforced accountability and reduced corruption by making traders act as agents of the government for indirect tax collection. Tax collections are in the range of Rs.40000 crores per annum through five-lakh returns and has eliminated one and a half lakh visits of traders daily to government offices. The KSWAN Network provides LAN and WAN services to all the Government offices across Karnataka. The Secretariat Local Area Network (SECLAN) is extensively used by the Karnataka Government Secretariat to run various e-Governance applications such as File Monitoring System, Letter Monitoring System and Attendance Monitoring System apart from Intranet and Internet. The Sachivalaya Vahini makes available various decisions taken online by the Government to the citizens. The Karnataka Resident Data Hub provides a "Single Source of Truth Platform" for all the departments to sanitize their databases and provide aadhaar based service delivery.

A similar eco-system at the sectoral level has been created in the Food and Civil Supplies department by the government of Karnataka jointly with the government of India. This includes establishment of electronic infrastructure for 212 offices and 312 PDS wholesale points that have been computerized and interlinked to a central server maintained by NIC; creation of a digitized dynamic ration card database with photo , biometric and demographic details of all the family members wherein new families can be added and the details of the existing families can be modified at any point of time; setting up a Transparency Portal ahara.kar.nic.in with comprehensive information on Ration Card status, details, and statistics, BPL criteria, FPS details, allotment details, office details, contact details, Acts & Rules; and status of online application and generation of electronic ration cards.

A third recent trend we see is the graduation to the next level in the evolutionary process of e-governance. Mobile One, by offering citizen services on mobile, overcomes limitations of e-access. It is India's first and the world's largest multi-mode mobile governance platform with a multitude of paid and free services- Push, Pull, Payment and Data Capture. Working on the principle of *ANYTIME, ANYWHERE, ANYHOW*, it ensures availability of G2C, B2C & G2B services 24x7x365 days at any location in India on any mobile device. Mobile One is a unified mobile platform for delivery of citizens' services by both the government and the private sector through an open platform; it can accept any service and is thus future-proof. As a platform integrated across all telecom operators, it works on the concept of delivering all its services through the 'One URL, One Short Code and One App' concept, so that the citizen can avail all the services under one access point, thus eliminating the need to visit multiple websites. Mobile one now service 50 plus departments, 650 services including payment of utilities and taxes. It is also useful for sending bulk messages by District Collectors for disaster management to alert government officers. Mobile One is Citizen-centric, making services available at the fingertips of people saves people the time and strain of having to stand in queues in all-weather to access government services. From a government department's point of view, having to look for various channels to provide citizen services through different vendors or service providers is a daunting task. Mobile One provides a one-stop shop for departments to just plug in their services which are already made available online without having a separate tendering process or managing SLAs with the vendors for service delivery and performance parameters.

An e-friendly eco system, the creation of which is a major responsibility of the government, encourages green shoots of social entrepreneurship using e-applications. Among the innovations by non- state actors, we may mention '3nethra,' a low-cost portable pre-screening ophthalmology device. The device can identify multiple diseases such as glaucoma, cataract, diabetic retina, refraction and cornea problems. It is promoted by a start-up which is among a new breed that builds affordable innovations for remote and poor areas in Karnataka and other parts of India, where large technology companies have failed to reach. Cardiotrack, a smartphone-sized ECG machine gives physicians all details needed to make a diagnosis. The ECG captured in a rural area can be instantaneously transferred to a cardiologist far away for interpretation, thus providing early diagnosis and prevention of heart diseases in rural and semi-urban areas. In the agriculture sector, NanoPix is an image and video processing technology that help farmers to sort agriculture products such as cashews by quality, shape, size and colour. It does not use expensive high-resolution cameras used in imaging technology. To keep the costs low, it combines the images from several low-cost cameras and uses software algorithm to create three dimensional models of the objects that need to be analysed.

I would therefore recommend some pre-caution in e-implementation of all kinds, not just governance alone. ICT is a tool of good governance, not an end in itself. It is important to realize that citizen satisfaction and welfare is effected not by ICT alone but by the combination of technology, organizational reform & social processes. All sustainable initiatives require a holistic approach to transform the ecosystem-standalone is not sustainable. Technology interventions are a convenience, not an ideology. And finally, value is generated not by technology but the way it is applied in a given context and this requires patience and humility in implementation.

Chapter 7
Green Supply Chain Management in Construction: A Multi-Theory Perspective

Sreejith Balasubramanian[1] Jacinta Dsilva[2]

[1]Middlesex University, Dubai-UAE.

[2]SEE Institute, Sustainable City, Dubai-UAE

Abstract

Green supply chain management (GSCM) has witnessed growing interest in recent times. However, most related studies are conceptual in nature and not sufficiently grounded in management theory. This forms the motivation for the present work where GSCM is sought to be analyzed and interpreted through the perspectives of different theoretical lenses. The focus is on the UAE construction sector, which accounts for roughly 30-40% of global greenhouse gas emissions and is complex due to interdependent activities across multiple stakeholders. Semi-structured interviews were conducted with all the key supply chain stakeholders along with supporting company documentation such as annual reports and departmental publications. The findings were interpreted through established (stakeholder theory, institutional theory, and resource-based-view) and emerging management theories (strategic choice theory, resource-dependence theory, complexity theory and legitimacy theory) from other disciplines. Very few GSCM studies in construction or other sectors have used management theories to explain the findings and this study contributes to that. The explanatory and predictive capability of theories used in this study will provide practitioners with a deeper conceptualization of GSCM perspectives beyond the individual issues in the supply chain.

Keywords: *Green supply chain management, construction sector, United Arab Emirates, Multi-theory perspectives*

1. Introduction

Green supply chain management (GSCM) has seen significant interest in recent years among both practitioners and researchers. However, despite the progress, GSCM is still finding it difficult to establish its own "distinct scientific identity" as a field of practice and as an academic domain and therefore is in danger of collapsing into a discredited management fad unless a reliable theoretical basis is developed (Touboulic and Walker, 2015). This lack of theoretical basis means, the generalizability and explanatory power of GSCM studies are constantly doubted, and therefore the findings obtained in a particular industry setting remain in that setting. Given the scientific notion that sound theoretical principles is fundamental for decision-making and managerial actions (Halldórsson et al., 2015), as well as advancement of any field, the main aim of this paper was to develop a higher-level abstraction of the GSCM concept with the use of established theories, especially from non-supply chain areas. However, given the broadness, one cannot rely on the use of one or two theories to explain the GSCM concept. Hence, this paper looks at GSCM from multiple theoretical perspectives depending on where and how the individual theories can, individually and in combination, contribute to providing a deeper, broader and simplistic conceptualization of GSCM perspectives. However, unlike other studies which made attempts to explain potential theories of GSCM from literature (Sarkis et al., 2011), this study attempts to reduce the gap between theory and practice and therefore use real data collected from two supply chain case studies. Given the sector's significant contribution to environmental degradation, construction sector was selected for this study.

The sector is responsible for one-third of global carbon emissions, one-third of global resource consumption, 40% of world's energy consumption, 40% of global waste generated, and 25% of the world's total water consumption (UNEP-SBCI, 2016, Balasubramanian and Shukla, 2017a). Despite these adverse environmental implications, construction vis-à-vis others sectors have seen limited application of GSCM (Malaviya and Kant, 2015; Balasubramanian and Shukla, 2017b), largely because of the sector's inherent complexity (interdependent activities across multiple stakeholders), and therefore, is expected to benefit largely from a theory enabled deeper and simplified understanding of GSCM. We have chosen United Arab Emirates (UAE) for the investigation, where the sector had taken significant strides in the past few years towards reducing the negative environmental impacts of the sector, which at one point was the highest in the world (Work bank report of UAE, 2008).

2. Literature review

The first objective of this review was to identify the key themes and constructs of GSCM, not only for a construction sector perspective but also in general. Identifying the critical themes and constructs is important, especially when there is a lack of agreement in relation to how the scope of GSCM is defined in literature (Ahi and Searcy, 2013). Therefore, GSCM related studies in construction in conjunction with other sector were carried out to understand the common themes and constructs.

From the review it was understood that the scope of GSCM revolved around four broad theoretical themes namely 1) what green practices do firms implement, and its extent of implementation; 2) what are the implications it (green practices) has on firm's performance; 3) what are the motives behind firms to implement such practices; 4) what barriers firms face implementing these practices. A closer examination of the themes enabled authors to sub-classify these themes into nine managerially relevant GSCM constructs. These robust theoretical constructs allow a deeper yet concise mapping of GSCM with theories. This theoretical construct identification is a contribution of the study given that construct development is at the core of theory building.

Using nine identified GSCM construct as its basis, the next phase of the review identified potential theories that could be used to explain these constructs in real world settings. Given that use of theories in empirical studies is scarce in the GSCM literature despite calls and various suggestions in the literature to use theories, we have also looked at SCM literature to inherit theories which we presumed to be of relevance to GSCM (Balasubramanian and Shukla, 2018). Several management theories were shortlisted including the three popular macro theories namely resource-based view (RBV), stakeholder theory and institutional theory.

However, before we conduct the empirical investigation to disentangle the rhetoric from the reality in terms of the theoretical underpinning of GSCM constructs, it is important to define a research approach and target respondents. Given the fact that greening of construction sector can only be effective if all the key supply chain stakeholders (SCS) are able to harmonize their conflicting interests and implement green practices in a coherent manner with other stakeholders in the supply chain, it is important to identify and categorize the key supply chain stakeholders. Stakeholder theory provides a strong conceptual basis for identifying and defining the key supply chain stakeholders, such as direct or indirect stakeholders, primary or secondary stakeholder (Delmas and Toffel, 2004). However, in context of supply chain management, these categorizations could be based on the core activities in the supply chain. On the basis, the key SCS of the sector are Developers, Architects/Consultants, Contractors and Suppliers, each having their own hierarchical position and activities in the supply chain.

3. Research Methodology

Using the proposed GSCM constructs as the conceptual basis, the research employs two separate case studies of end to end supply chains to investigate the different green aspects of individual supply chain stakeholders. A case study approach was selected since they are more effective where the theory is still emerging. The two case studies differ in the fact that in one of the supply chain, all the key supply chain firms involved are large firms (Case A), while in the other are small/medium firms (Case B). We have purposefully selected the contrasting supply chains by firm size in order to stretch the explanatory power of the underlying theories, the raison d'etre of good theories is that it should be able to explain contrasting scenarios with relative ease. Each case study involved multiple, semi-structured interviews with key firms in the supply chain. A total of 21 interviews across 12 firms (7 in case A and 5 in Case B) was conducted. Kvale (2007) and Rabionet (2011) were used as a base for developing ethical guidelines and interview protocols. The interviews were recorded, transcribed, and checked with respondents for accuracy and then analyzed. Further, any supporting company documentation such as annual reports, and departmental publications were also analyzed to complement the findings.

4. Analysis and Findings

Stakeholder analysis (which can also be seen as an application of stakeholder theory) was conducted to understand the commonalities and differences that exist in practice with respect to GSCM constructs and its sub-aspects across supply chain stakeholders. The theoretical mappings of constructs based on the empirical study are as follows:

4.1. Drivers of green practices

These are factors that influence firms to implement green practices. It is classified as external or internal, depending on the origin of these drivers (Walker et al., 2008).

External drivers are pressures faced by firms from outside entities such a governments, competitors, consumers and non-governmental organization (NGO's). Institutional theory provides a theoretical lens for classifying these external pressures. According to the theory, firms are under constant coercive pressure to adapt to (implement green practice) and be consistent with their external institutional environment.

In the case of the UAE, the findings show that the main coercive pressure faced by Developers are from the government in the form of stringent green building regulations and associated fines and penalties. In the case of Architects/Consultants, the coercive pressure occurs not from governments but from Developer. For instance, pre-qualification criteria for Architects to participate in tender now include stringent environmental criteria. In addition, green design competitions are also conducted by Developers to award the design contract to Architects/Consultants. In the case of Contractors, they face coercive pressure from both governments such as implementing mandatory onsite waste management practices and from Developers on an array of green aspects in terms of pre-qualification and tender specifications. Interestingly, the main material suppliers (e.g.: steel, aluminium, glass, cement) face little or no coercive pressure from governments and other supply chain stakeholders.

Overall, it can be generalized that for larger firms, the influence of institutional drivers on the implementation of green practices is much higher than small firms, as they consider these institutional pressures very seriously, whereas smaller firms struggle to cope with these institutional pressures (Khan et al., 2022).

Internal drivers are pressures that arise from within the organization to implement green practices. These can be either due to a firm's environmental commitment or/and for achieving clearly identified business benefits (Varnas et al., 2009). The main internal drivers identified from the case study include firms environmental commitment, cost savings, improving brand reputation and entering foreign markets. Environmental commitment of firms can be perceived as a voluntary obligation to society and can be explained from an institutional theoretic perspective namely mimetic cultural-cognitive isomorphism, a rational desire to embrace green practices that is consistent with the obligations and values of the society in which they function (Hsu et al., 2013). The findings from the interview confirm this mimetic cultural-cognitive isomorphism as firms (mainly large firms) green practices are influenced by their environmental commitment, which according to the respondents is either inspired by other firms in the UAE or abroad, or because of the values of their owners/top management. However, this commitment was clearly high among large firms and was far beyond what was required to meet the institutional pressures. Potential cost savings from green practices was seen as a driver for Contractors and Suppliers, especially among large ones to implement green practices.

Barriers of green practices

These are factors that prevent firms from implementing green practices. It is also classified as external or internal, depending on the origin of these barriers (Walker et al., 2008).

External Barriers are barriers that are beyond the firm's control. The main barriers identified from the study that adversely impacts the implementation of green practices are a shortage of green professionals, shortage of green suppliers, tight and inflexible stakeholder deadlines and lack of stakeholder engagement. The first two barriers were highlighted by all stakeholders except suppliers across both the supply chains and can be explained using resource-dependence theory. According to the theory (Pfeffer and Salancik, 1978), organizations are dependent on resources (material and human resources) provided by outside parties to compete (implementation of green practices). The theory also warrants the need for establishing inter-organizational collaboration and the establishment of formal and semi-formal linkages with other firms to ensure strategically critical resources are available.

Internal Barriers are barriers that arise from within the organization. Two important barriers identified from the case study are a lack of knowledge and awareness and the high cost of implementation. The findings indicate that lack of knowledge and awareness was more of a concern for Developers and Contractors compared to Architects/Consultants and Suppliers, though the moderating impact of firm size was evident across all firms, with larger firms having relatively higher knowledge and awareness than small firms. Regarding the high cost of implementation involved with green projects was a major concern for Developers in both the supply chains. Similarly, the high capital investment required for green manufacturing as a barrier was highlighted by large and small Suppliers. For Architects/Consultants, the high cost of implementation (such as the implementation of state-of-the-art green design tools) as a barrier was highlighted by a small firm. Both, these barriers can be explained from a RBV theoretical perspective.

4.2. Green practices

These are practices carried out by organizations to minimize the negative environmental effects. The case study identified the relevant green practices of each stakeholder.

Core green practices are practices implemented at the supply chain level, covering each of the major stages. The main practices include environmental impact assessment, green design, green purchasing, green transportation, green construction/green manufacturing (in the case of suppliers) and end of life management. However, it was evident from the case study that not all stakeholders were involved in all the stages. For example, green construction was not relevant for Developer and Architect/Consultant. Similarly, Contractors are not involved at the design stage and therefore green design is not relevant for them.

Facilitating green practices are practices implemented at the organizational level to develop a conducive environment for green practices to be implemented at supply chain level. The important practices implemented across all stakeholders as evident from the case study include environmental management systems (EMS) and ISO 14001, environmental training and auditing, cross-functional integration of departments and functions for implementing green practices, and green related research and development (R&D).

5. Conclusion

The contributions of the study are manyfold. First, it posits several managerially relevant constructs to define the scope of GSCM. Secondly, drawing on the analysis using real case data, the study uses several management theories to explain the GSCM phenomenon and integrate it into a larger body of knowledge. Thirdly, given the theoretical underpinning, from a practitioner's perspective, the insights obtained from the UAE construction sector context can be broadly generalized to other geographical and industry contexts. In terms of novelty, to the best of our knowledge, this is the first overarching study in the field of GSCM that uses multiple theories to explain the real findings obtained from a complex industry setting. In terms of research implications, the study shows that we cannot rely on one or two theoretical explanations (e.g. stakeholder theory, RBV etc.) to explain the GSCM concept. Though overlapping, there is a need to consider several theories and depending on the context, researchers can choose one or two theories as the dominant ones and others as supporting ones. Very few GSCM studies in construction have used management theories to explain the findings and this study contributes to that. The main limitation is that the theories presented in the study are by no means exhaustive and the theories used could be biased based on the author's knowledge of various theories. Future researchers could explore new theories/underpin some of the proposed theories in different industry/country settings. Overall, we believe this paper significantly contributes towards developing GSCM as an established scientific discipline.

Reference

Ahi, P. & Searcy, C. (2013), 'A comparative literature analysis of definitions for green and sustainable supply chain management', *Journal of Cleaner Production*, Vol. 52, pp.329-341.

Balasubramanian, S., & Shukla, V. (2017a). Green supply chain management: an empirical investigation on the construction sector. Supply Chain Management: An International Journal, 22(1), 58-81.

Balasubramanian, S., & Shukla, V. (2017b). Green supply chain management: the case of the construction sector in the United Arab Emirates (UAE). Production Planning & Control, 28(14), 1116-1138.

Balasubramanian, S., & Shukla, V. (2018). Environmental supply chain management in the construction sector: Theoretical underpinnings. International Journal of Logistics Research and Applications, 21(5), 502-528.

Delmas, M. & Toffel, M. W. (2004), 'Stakeholders and environmental management practices: an institutional framework. Business strategy and the Environment', Vol. 13, No. 4, pp. 209-222.

Hsu, C. C., Choon Tan, K., Hanim Mohamad Zailani, S. & Jayaraman, V. (2013), 'Supply chain drivers that foster the development of green initiatives in an emerging economy', *International Journal of Operations & Production Management*, Vol. 33, No. 6, pp. 656-688.

Khan, S., Ali, S. and Singh, R. (2022). Determinants of Remanufacturing Adoption for Circular Economy: A Causal Relationship Evaluation Framework, *Applied System Innovation,* 5(4), 62. https://doi.org/10.3390/asi5040062.

Khan, S., Singh, R. and Kirti. (2021). Critical Factors for Blockchain Technology Implementation: A Supply Chain Perspective, *Journal of Industrial Integration and Management,* 2150011.
https://doi.org/10.1142/s2424862221500111.

Khan, S., Singh, R., Haleem, A., Dsilva, J. and Ali, S. (2022). Exploration of Critical Success Factors of Logistics 4.0: A DEMATEL Approach, *Logistics,* 6(1), 13.
https://doi.org/10.3390/logistics6010013.

Kvale, S. (2007), Doing interviews, *Sage, Thousand Oaks*, CA.

Post, J. E., Preston, L. E. & Sachs, S. (2002), 'Managing the extended enterprise: The new stakeholder view', California *management review*, Vol. 45, No. 1, pp. 6-28.

Pachar, S., Singh, R. and Wahid, M. (2021). Implication of Renewable Energy in Sustainable Development in India: Future Strategy, *IOP Conference Series: Material Science and Engineering,* 1149(1), 012020. https://doi.org/10.1088/1757-899x/1149/1/012020.

Pachar, S., Singh, R.(2021). Role of Sustainable development goals and corporate social responsibility in India's growth: opportunities and challenges, *Empirical Economics Letters*, 20(2), 277-281.

Rabionet, S. E. (2011), 'How I Learned to Design and Conduct Semi-structured Interviews: An Ongoing and Continuous Journey', *The Qualitative Report*, Vol. 16 No. 2, pp. 563-566.

Salancik, G. R. & Pfeffer, J. (1978), 'The external control of organizations: A resource dependence perspective', *Harper & Row*, New York.

Singh, R et al. (2022). Quality 4.0 in Healthcare: Application of the EFQM Excellence Mode. *Empirical Economics Letters,* 21(2), 1-19.

Singh, R. (2018). The Cause of Unemployment in Current Market Scenario, *Vivechan International Journal of Research,* 9(1), 86-81.

Singh, R., DSilva, J. and Kumar, R. S. (2021). Modelling the CSR Initiatives on Firm Performance: A Context of Emerging Economies, *Empirical Economic Letters,* 20 (3), 221-228.

Singh, R., Dsilva, J., Centobelli, P. and Tripathi, V. (2021). A review on Sustainable HRM: A study evaluating Sustainability for organisational development, The Empirical Economics Letters, 20(2), 1-10.

Singh, R., Khan, S. and Dsilva, J. (2022). A framework for assessment of critical factor for circular economy practice implementation, *Journal of Modelling in Management*, https://doi.org/10.1108/jm2-06-2021-0145.

Singh, S, Singh, R, Shandilya, T and Kumar, R.S. (2021). Digital security issues in emerging technology management, *Empirical Economics Letters,* 20(5), 205-213.

Touboulic, A. & Walker, H. (2015), 'Theories in sustainable supply chain management: a structured literature review', *International Journal of Physical Distribution & Logistics Management*, Vol. 45, No. 1/2, pp. 16-42.

UNEP-SBCI (2016), available at http://www.unep.org/sbci/AboutSBCI/Background.asp (accessed 28 March 2016)

Varnäs, A., Balfors, B. & Faith-Ell, C. (2009), 'Environmental consideration in procurement of construction contracts: current practice, problems and opportunities in green procurement in the Swedish construction industry', *Journal of Cleaner Production,* Vol. 17 No. 3, pp. 1214-1222.

Walker, H., Di Sisto, L. & McBain, D. (2008), 'Drivers and barriers to environmental supply chain management practices: lessons from the public and private sectors', *Journal of Purchasing and Supply Management*, Vol 14, No. 1, pp. 69-85.

World Bank (2008), 'Country Report of UAE', available at http://data.worldbank.org/country/united-arab-emirates (accessed 28 March 2016).

Chapter 8
Talent Management during Industry 4.0: A Viewpoint

Sucheta Agarwal[1], Jitendra Kumar Dixit[1] and Vivek Agrawal[1]

[1]Institute of Business Management, GLA University, Mathura, India

Abstract

Businesses have a greater responsibility to anticipate future skill requirements when the environment is becoming dynamic because of fast technology and organizational change. It causes major skill and knowledge shortages in the business sector and engenders transformation. In the era of Industry 4.0, talent management is a basis of competitive advantage that firms can no longer ignore. It goes hand in hand with locating, cultivating, and retaining A-level performers. In the context of Industry 4.0, this may require investing more time and resources in a nonexistent talent war. In light of this, the present study presented the viewpoint of talent management and its related aspects during Industry 4.0. This study will help academics and researchers figure out how to improve the system for managing talent.

Keywords: Career Management, Talent, Talent Enlargement, Talent Fascination, Talent management, Industry 4.0

1. Introduction

Academics, businesses, and practitioners frequently highlight the difficulties that come with managing talent in contemporary labor markets, but the literature on the issue is scant and has developed somewhat haphazardly. But because of the unparalleled speed and scope of change brought about by Industry 4.0, technology is already exceeding people's and organizations' capacity for adaptation (Al Amiri and Abu Shawali, 2021; Deloitte, 2017). The Fourth Industrial Revolution changes our personal and professional lives. Technological developments comparable to the first, second, and third industrial revolutions permit new advanced human development episodes. These innovations are combining with the environmental, physical, digital, and biological worlds to develop great promise for creativity and risk. This revolution's speed, breadth, and depth are driving us to reconsider our country's development, organizational value creation, and even human psychology development. The Fourth Industrial Revolution is more than just technology-driven change; it is a chance to enable leaders, policymakers, and people from all socioeconomic levels and nations to leverage converging technologies to create an inclusive, human-centered future. Therefore, it is imperative to investigate how well-suited current talent management theory and practice are for this situation (Mujtaba et al., 2022). The global market of today is fast-moving, dynamic, uncertain, and extremely competitive. As a result, businesses all over the world are confronting significant decisions and issues in the area of talent management (Khilji et al., 2015; Schuler et al., 2011). Management of people, especially high-potential employees and knowledge workers, is a growing strategic concern for businesses worldwide (Mujtaba et al., 2022). Since McKinsey consultants popularized the expression "the fight for talent" in the late 1990s to emphasize the role leaders and high potentials play in guiding firms' success, top managers and academics have shown an increasing interest in talent management. This curiosity has been growing for a while (McDonnell, 2011).

This article has placed an emphasis on the examination of the conceptual aspects of talent management as well as the concepts that are related to those aspects. This study would provide future direction, both qualitatively and quantitatively, to the researchers who are focusing on this particular field. Hence, the research objective of this study is:

RO: To investigate and discuss the concept of talent management and its related concepts.

The methodology part has been discussed after the explanation of the introduction section. Furthermore, this study discussed the theoretical background of talent management and its related concepts. Lastly, the conclusion part was discussed with the elaboration of limitations and future scope of the study.

2. Methodology of the study

This perspective on the talent management system during Industry 4.0 has addressed the previous studies or articles. This paper shows what the authors thought about the talent management system after looking at a lot of studies on it. It also talks about the limitations of the study and where it could go in the future.

3. Talent management: A viewpoint

Since there is no widely accepted definition for the term "talent management," nearly every article on the topic starts with a discussion of its conceptual limitations. For instance, Lewis & Heckman (2006, p. 139) describe a "worrisome lack of clarity regarding the definition, scope, and ultimate aims of talent management." Similarly, Collings et al. (2009, p. 1264) find that "the idea of talent management lacks definition, theoretical development, and empirical evidence." Gallardo-Gallo et al. (2013, p. 291) say, "It seems that talent can mean anything a business leader or writer wants it to mean, since everyone has their own idea of what it includes and what it doesn't."

The goal of talent management is to attract and keep the best talent from employees, which is essential for business expansion. In order for a business to prepare to deal with future skills shortfalls, talent management is the systematic process of finding, employing, developing, keeping, and rewarding exceptional people (Collings et al., 2015). Fear of a talent shortage is a global problem as well. All businesses compete globally for the same talent. To ensure an industrial edge, the global integration movement exemplifies standardization in hiring, management, and people development. 4.0.

4. Industry 4.0 and Talent Management

Germany Trade and Invest, GTAI (2011, p. 6) defines Industry 4.0 as "the technical development from embedded systems to cyber-physical systems that enables technologies like Internet of Things and online data and services to build a genuinely networked world." According to Bayraktar and Atac (2018), Industry 4.0 will destroy certain occupations, create new ones, shift critical skills, and create new methods of thinking about and running a business (Al Amiri and Abu Shawali, 2021). World Economic Forum, WEF (2019) highlighted Industry 4.0 labor capabilities. These skills include 1) developing new leadership abilities, such as the ability to embrace ambiguity and explain risks and uncertainties to the workforce; 2) combining operational management, technology, integration, and people management skills; and 3) using analytic, problem-solving, and critical thinking abilities. Improving employee experience, creating an agile and personalized learning culture, developing metrics for valuing human capital, and incorporating diversity and inclusion into the workplace. Shaw and Varghese (2018) predict that the Internet of Things, big data, and artificial intelligence will automate the majority of HR-related tasks and that HR departments will take on a more strategic role in the competitiveness of organizations. To succeed in Industry 4.0, managers need to be innovative and have strong management skills. Whysall et al. (2019) contend that talent management theory and practice should evolve to reflect a more systemic, dynamic attitude.

5. Talent Management: Related Concepts

5.1. Talent Management Stratagem

Integrating and harmonizing talent management plans with organizational strategies is crucial, as is articulating talent management strategies. Talent management is related to the organization's culture and personnel. When employee goals are aligned with corporate goals, the organization's goals and objectives are realized and the business benefits.

5.2. Talent Fascination

The initial approach in talent management is the recruitment of highly qualified people who will become future leaders of the firm. There are both internal and external sources for employee resources (O'Bryan & Casey, 2017). There are a number of factors to consider when an organization promotes from within, including the fact that employees already have insight and knowledge of the organization's business processes and that the motivation of employees who are assigned to new roles is higher.

However, if the business wants to implement a new change, it is preferable to recruit employees from outside the organization. The best way to get the best potential employees is for a organization to have a good reputation in the community. This can be done through public relations, organization branding, organization introduction, corporate social responsibility, and promotion. All the aspects are important for building the organizational image in the present competitive market during

Industry 4.0 (Pagan-Castaño et al., 2022); Wiblen & Marler, 2021).

5.3. Talent Enlargement

Talent enlargement is an important aspect of employee growth, namely how firms grow individuals with their unique capacities for creativity, information acquisition, and job motivation. Businesses can use a variety of talent development (enlargement) programs to improve employees' skills, attitudes, and knowledge in order to improve their performance.

Talent development includes the instruments of training and development, mentoring, coaching, and succession planning. Talent is an ability that may be developed through acquiring knowledge and practice. As companies continue to use new technology, business models, and market strategies, it is important that their employees' skills are always improving.

5.4. Talent Maintenance

The purpose of talent maintenance (retention) is to retain employees at periods of peak performance. Talent turnover and attrition is extremely risky for a business since it needs a significant investment in recruiting new talent and aligning them with the organization's objectives. This includes recruitment costs, transition costs, indirect costs connected with new ideas, lower productivity, etc. as well effect on the image of the organization.

Keeping talented people on board is important and should be one of the organization's main duties if it wants to stay competitive through the skills and abilities of its employees (O'Bryan & Casey, 2017). There are two factors that can encourage employees to remain with an organization: intrinsic and extrinsic incentives. Intrinsic motivations pertain to monetary items that can meet employees' physiological needs, such as appealing compensation packages and additional incentives such as medical schemes, family tours or related vacation leaves etc. Extrinsic incentives are things like flexible work hours, recognition, inclusive working environment etc., that can be mentally rewarding but don't have to do with money (Bonneton et al., 2022). These are the strategies of the organization to keep retain the talented employee by build a "people-first" culture

5.5. Career Management

Career management or development and planning focus on staff growth and development through rotation, transfer, promotion, employee workshops, and an employee care program. Career management can improve employee performance, retention, and attendance (Bonneton et al., 2022). This enhances the employee's personality and prepares them for the future.

5.6. Employees with Talent

Talented employees have added value for stakeholders. Not only are they qualified and knowledgeable about their work, but they can also handle any business problems that may arise. They can be become as an intrapreneurs to encourage the creativity and innovation in the working environment of the organization (Al-Dalahmeh and Héder-Rima, 2021).

5.7. Talent as a Manifestation

If the entire process and system align with the organization's objectives, the firm will continue to function. Talented human capital performs these functions; hence it is crucial that talent management 4.0 is integrated with the organization's business plan in order to acquire a competitive edge over rivals (Amankwah-Amoah., 2018). The organization utilizes this skill to solve problems and uncover vulnerabilities that may be remedied and turned into a competitive advantage. If an organization wants to be successful, it needs to put money into managing its employees' skills.

6. Conclusion

This study demonstrates that talent management is crucial for the survival of for-profit companies during the industry 4.0. In this era of artificial intelligence, labor mobility is quite high, not only across national borders but also internationally, making talent management challenges crucial as many enterprises and nations compete for skilled individuals. Incorporating the new technologies that make employees more competitive, a talent management system may be utilized to optimize the performance of each individual and the entire organization. Because there is a visionary concept, ambitious goals, and inventive production, a organization's primary source of profit is its skilled workers. Talent management is now a crucial corporate component that decides and shapes a new human management strategy. The purpose of this viewpoint is to give a fundamental approach to talent management, as several firms still do not comprehend its practice and learning process for the development of the employees in the era of Industry 4.0.

When people are successful, businesses are successful as well. Employers who cultivate a culture that encourages their workers to be their best and helps them achieve their full potential are more likely to see improvements in employee and organizational performance (Hongal and Kinange, 2020; Saleh and Atan, 2021). Businesses can become employers of choice and draw people organically in today's fiercely competitive marketplace by making their brand a key element of their talent strategy (Lewis and Heckman, 2006). Unexpected departures leave gaps in coverage, but a talent pipeline makes it easy to fill those gaps quickly and keep operations running smoothly.

Incessant coaching/mentoring that focuses on employees' strengths helps them learn new skills and reach their full potential.

7. Implications

Talent management 4.0 explains the interaction of talent management with technology. This technology incorporation into the organization's functions gives the big picture of advancement, development, and growth in both tangible and intangible aspects. This study focused on the various related aspects of talent management 4.0. Some implications of this study are as follows:

• Talent management 4.0 facilitates the formulation of business strategies to manage and retain the talent in the organization. This helps in maintaining the competitive edge in the market to remain progressive and sustainably in the VUCA (Volatility, Uncertainty, Complexity, Ambiguity) world.

• The practice of succession planning is an important part of talent management 4.0 because it contributes to the development of a trained labor force that is able to fulfil leadership and other crucial responsibilities as the company expands, transforms, or develops. When there is growth in an organization or a change in management, succession planning helps to guarantee that productivity and employee morale, are not negatively impacted.

The talent management 4.0, makes appropriate matching between job and the candidate. You will have a better chance of succeeding in your function if the content of the job is attractive to you, taking into account both your interests and your personality. As part of continuous HR efforts, this kind of best practice can be ensured by a competent talent management

References

Hongal, P. and Kinange, U. (2020), "A Study on Talent Management and its Impact on Organization Performance- An Empirical Review", International Journal of Engineering and Management Research, 10 (1), 64-71

Khilji, S. E., Tarique, I., & Schuler, R. S. (2015). Incorporating the macro view in global talent management. *Human resource management review*, *25*(3), 236-248.

Lewis RE & Heckman RJ. 2006. Talent management: a critical review. Hum. Resour.Manag. Rev. 16(2):139–54

McDonnell, A. (2011), "Still fighting the 'war for talent'? Bridging the science versus practice gap", Journal of Business and Psychology, Vol. 26 No. 2, pp. 169-73

Mujtaba, M., Mubarik, M.S. and Soomro, K.A. (2022), "Measuring talent management: a proposed construct", *Employee Relations*, Vol. 44 No. 5, pp. 1192-1215.

O'Bryan, C., & Casey, A. M. (2017). Talent management: hiring and developing engaged employees. *Library Leadership & Management*, *32*(1), 1-17.

Pagan-Castaño, E., Ballester-Miquel, J. C., Sánchez-García, J., & Guijarro-García, M. (2022). What's next in talent management?. *Journal of Business Research*, *141*, 528-535.

Saleh, R., & Atan, T. (2021). The Involvement of Sustainable Talent Management Practices on Employee's Job Satisfaction: Mediating Effect of Organizational Culture. *Sustainability*, *13*(23), 1-17.

Schuler, R.S., Jackson, S.E. and Tarique, I. (2011), "Global talent management and global talent challenges: strategic opportunities for IHRM", Journal of World Business, Vol. 46, pp. 506-16.

Shaw, P., & Varghese, R. M. (2018). Industry 4.0 and Future of HR. Journal of Management, 5(6), 96-103.

Wiblen, S., & Marler, J. H. (2021). Digitalised talent management and automated talent decisions: the implications for HR professionals. *The International Journal of Human Resource Management, 32*(12), 2592-2621.

Whysall, Z., Owtram, M. and Brittain, S. (2019), "The new talent management challenges of Industry 4.0", Journal of Management Development, Vol. 38 No. 2, pp. 118-129.

World Economic Forum. (2019). HR4.0: shaping people strategies in the fourth industrial revolution. Retrieved February 29, 2020 from http://www3.weforum.org/ docs/WEF_NES_Whitepaper_ HR4.0.pdf

Chapter 9
Impact of Industry 4.0 on Supply Chain Management

Ashish Kumar Gupta[1], Aditya Rane[1], Amit Choudhari [2], Ashutosh Gupta[3],

Prathamesh Sapale[4], and Rajmohan Muthaiah[5]

[1]School of Mechanical and Aerospace Engineering, Oklahoma State University, Stillwater, OK, USA

[2]Cleveland State University, Cleveland, OH, USA

[3]Dayanand Vedic College, Orai, UP, India

[4]Vignan's Foundation for Science, Technology and Research, Guntur, AP, India

[5]School of Aerospace and Mechanical Engineering, University of Oklahoma, Norman, OK, USA

Abstract: The present work gives an overview of the modern technologies utilized in industry 4.0 that can be effectively utilized in supply chain management systems to improve efficiency through the utilization of artificial intelligence, machine learning, the Internet of things, and machine learning. The Internet of Things has dramatically expanded in many industries, necessitating the deployment of artificial intelligence tools for the best possible data utilization. Combining these technologies allows for more dynamic cost, automation, and productivity reduction.

Keywords: Supply chain management, Internet of things, Artificial intelligence, Machine learning, Operational research

1 Introduction

Nowadays, Companies are required to take advantage of any worthwhile opportunity to enhance their business operations in the current highly competitive climate that is distinguished by exquisite consumer demands for high-quality goods and services with a narrow profit margin (Lee & Lee, 2015). The basic challenge of supply chain management (SCM) is to maintain a steady inflow of goods, information, services, and financial inputs while cutting costs (Leung et al., 2007). There is a need to digitally transform the enterprise process to realize the vision of industry 4.0. The present condition of the supply chain is a series of largely distinct steps taken through product development, manufacturing, distribution, and finally into the hands of the customer. The close function includes integrated planning and execution systems, visibility, autonomous logistics, smart procurement and warehousing, spare parts management, and advanced analytics (Manavalan & Jayakrishna, 2019). Dramatic advent in computer processing motivates the organization to innovate digital technology and capabilities that make the organization incorporate industry 4.0 (Hiromoto et al.).

The purpose of this study is to gather the best research to aid in developing a conceptual framework that integrates IoT and AI, Machine learning and cloud computing technologies into modern supply chain management with a focus on logistics management. Furthermore, the role of the 5G network is carefully examined to reveal its potential and the processing power that it may offer to the IoT and AI activities by using recent data published globally.

2 Background of Supply chain 4.0

Supply chain 4.0 is an advanced version of the supply chain that facilitates distinct Industry 4.0 technologies for instance

Internet of things (IoT), the Cloud, Artificial intelligence (AI), and Big Data. Furthermore, the combination of advanced AI algorithms, business intelligence tools, data sciences, and other next-gen technologies substantially ameliorate supply chain management (de Vass et al., 2021). Therewithal, the IoT forms an integrated network between different supply chain management (SCM) and logistics activities, enabling enterprises to track shipments and making it possible to automate workflows. In addition, it permits the organization to work against numerous challenges accompanied by traditional SCM networks and builds resilience and a responsive supply Chain system.

1.   Integration of physical to digital signal – Signal is captured from the physical world to create a digital record.

2.   Link between digital to digital – Sharing of information using advanced analytics, Artificial intelligence provides meaningful insights.

3.   Relation between Digital to Physical – information delivery takes place through automated and more effective ways to give rise to actions that create changes in the physical world.

3   Supply Chain 4.0 Ecosystem:

The traditional supply chain follows the standardized process, Marketing personnel analyses the trends of customer demands and tries to predict sales for the future period this information is helpful for manufacturers to order the raw materials, components, and parts to fulfill the anticipated production capacity. The technique of forecasting cannot always be treated as the validated source of information there are always possibilities of inconsistency. Lack of communication in the supply chain has a negative impact on the players who are involved in the supply chain network.

As shown in fig. 1, the supply chain 4.0 ecosystem utilizes Artificial Intelligence for automatizing the entire supply chain, Cloud computing, and data analysis to do the complex analysis so that future demands can be predicted more precisely. Operational research acts as a refinement tool that can be used to optimize the infinite number of possible solutions obtained during cloud computing and select the best possible solution to reduce the load on the manufacturer, supplier, and waiting for the time of the product to be delivered to the customer end. IoT is becoming popular nowadays because of its usefulness and easy to adaptable nature to the current working system or machines. It plays an important role in collecting the data virtually and keeps continuous communication between the players involved in the supply chain network.

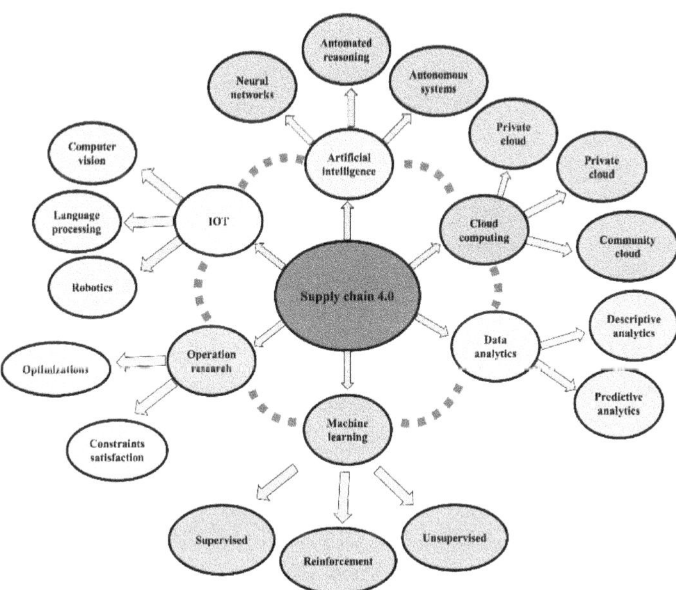

Figure 1. Schematic representation of the Supply chain 4.0 ecosystem.

3.1 Traditional supply chain model vs Digitalized supply chain Ecosystem.

The process of the traditional supply chain is demonstrated in fig. 2, which starts with the supply and ends with the customer.

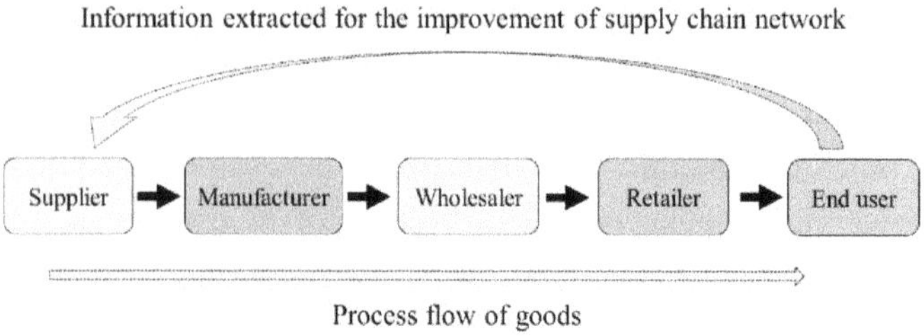

Figure 2. Demonstrate the traditional supply chain model.

While the traditional supply chain only concentrates on manufacturing and provision, the modern (digital) supply chain also attempts to increase the value of the product that is provided to the client, rather than merely concentrating on the distribution component. In contrast to the old supply chain, which allows listed firms to pursue a particular path, the modern (digital) supply chain enables every corporate organization to enjoy the value of forging partnerships. Compared to the conventional supply chain, the modern (digital) supply chain enables quicker advancement (Gu & Jing). The process is made sure to be effective and efficient, and the goods are delivered safely. For example in case of HVAC (Talkar et al., 2020) ducts, pipes, filters, building envelops (Choudhari et al., 2021) etc. ordered by the customer can be easily automated. The digital supply chain places more emphasis on forming alliances, partnerships, and collaborations. Businesses can develop trust and long-lasting connections with their suppliers by improving their ties with them.

3.1.1 Receiving Raw Materials:

Raw materials are collected from the supplier in order to process the final product. The manufacturer collects all the raw materials to make the final product.

3.1.2 Manufacturing Process:

The manufacturer then initiates the manufacturing process various types of equipment are involved to assemble the final product. The raw materials undergo various manufacturing processes to get transformed into the final product.

3.1.3 Wholesaler and Retailer distribution:

Once the quality product has been manufactured it is sent to the wholesalers whose responsibility is to distribute the products in predetermined quantities to the retailers. Retailers play significant roles in the distribution of the product to the customer.

3.1.4 Consumption by the end customers:

The final stage of the traditional supply chain is the delivering the product to the customer and taking the feedback so that this data may be utilized for any improvement in the product functionality or safety. For example delivering the vacuum fryer (Gupta et al.) machine or mini CNC machine parts (Choudhari et al., 2020) by the supplier to the customers.

3.2 Drawbacks

The above process shows the working of the traditional supply chain, as multiple stages are involved in the supply chain it comes with the following drawbacks.

1. Limited visibility throughout the supply chain – Lack of communication between the intermediate stages engenders limited transparency in the traditional supply chain ecosystem

2.   Lack of real-time data update – Real-time monitoring becomes difficult because there is no end-to-end connection between the players involved in the process of the supply chain for instance live tracking of inventory at the distributor's location is impossible hence carrying out a replenishment cycle at regular intervals becomes difficult.

3.   More expected delays.

4.   Cannot adapt or less responsive to changing market conditions.

On the other side, the modern supply chain isn't even a chain at all; rather, it's a fluid, agile value network created to offer instant choice and hyper-personalization across numerous fulfillment routes and a growing number of digital enablers. The conventional method of producing the same product in big quantities for merchants and distributors is no longer used. Companies are now altering the ways in which they manage their supply networks. The transfer of goods and services from one business to another during the development of supply chain management involved a combination of manual and computer-driven operations. This is moving too slowly in an era where new items have shorter life cycles.

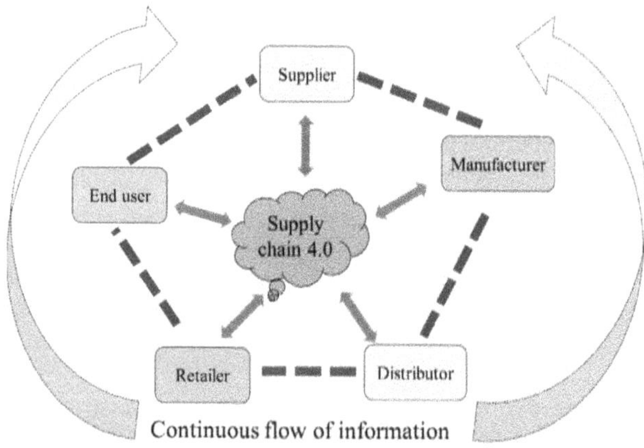

Figure 3. Demonstrate the model of digital Supply chain 4.0.

There is a shift toward an inflection point in how a firm responds to supply chain demands from its consumers due to the demand for "Faster, Cheaper, Better." Businesses are seeking for a means to speed up time to market and automate the purchasing process. Moving to a fully digital environment speeds up a business's time to market while also enhancing quality, cost-cutting efforts, and customer happiness. The modern supply chain is a network of suppliers created to offer immediate selection, hyper-personalization, and a variety of fulfillment routes and digital enablers (Dutta & Mitra, 2021). In order to provide ongoing planning capabilities and automatic responses to predetermined situations, a successful supply network makes use of data-driven intelligent automation systems like artificial intelligence (AI) and machine learning (ML). The system can be trained to differentiate between minor changes and circumstances that call for re-planning, which results in shorter planning cycles and the capacity to react to demand and supply dynamics more quickly.

Application Program Interfaces, or APIs, provide computer-driven supply chain solutions by providing better access into suppliers' systems as the industry transitions to a digital supply chain (Zahedi et al., 2021). They can compare their needs with a supplier's capacity to meet them using this real-time data to make an informed choice. a website serving as the first node in the Supply Chain of Things (SCoT). Investigating and using some of these approaches can give businesses exponential advantages in their processes.

4   Discussion

The concept of a supply chain existed long before the products themselves and is as old as the products themselves. The supply chain is a complex and integrated concept that encompasses the entire production and distribution channels, beginning with suppliers and ending with the end customer. The supply chain's goals are typical to meet customer demand, improve responsiveness, and establish a network among various stakeholders. The supply chain network is becoming more distributed, diverse, and transparent in terms of its business structure, business tasks, and stakeholders (Seyedghorban et al., 2020). For many organizations, the main issue is that the visibility of the entire supply chain and the level of information available within the organization are not optimal. As a result, the goal of Supply Chain Management (SCM) with AI and IoT is to digitalize the business process, integrate various stakeholders and assets, and achieve total system competitive advantage goals (Tammela et al., 2008). Many industries have recently become more interested in the potential applications of Artificial Intelligence (AI) technology (Dubey et al., 2020). AI is the ability of machines to learn from experience and make decisions based on a series of performances as intelligent as a human (Duan et al., 2019). Many major players in the technology industry, including Amazon, Walmart, Philips, eBay, and others, have made efforts to implement AI in SCM (Mahroof, 2019).

The advancement of information technology, particularly the internet, has altered the market's demand and supply framework.

All aspects of Supply chain management (SCM) have become more complex, and we cannot rely solely on past experience. This resulted in the creation of the industrial internet of things (IIoT) and industry 4.0. To comprehend IIoT, we must first comprehend the internet of things (IoT). IoT is the interconnection of computing devices embedded in everyday objects via the internet, allowing them to send and receive data.

The "Internet of Things," as previously stated, is the most promising foundation for Intelligent SCM. The term "Internet of Things" was coined in 1999 as the title of a presentation given by K. Ashton at Procter & Gamble (P&G) that linked the new concept of RFID in P&G's supply chain to the then-hot topic of the Internet (Ashton, 2009). The main idea of K. Ashton's IoT meaning is that we need to provide computers with their own means of gathering information so that they can "see," "hear," and "smell" the world for themselves. RFID and sensor technology allow computers to observe, identify, and comprehend the world without the constraints of manually entered data (Evtodieva et al., 2020).

Benefits of these activities for SCM include more accurate product tracking, faster delivery, and more efficient storage.

According to IOT Analytics' research (Fig:-1), there will be more than 25 billion IoT devices on the planet by 2025.The Internet of Things market is expected to grow 18% to 14.4 billion active connections by 2022. It is expected that there will be approximately 27 billion connected IoT devices by 2025, as supply constraints ease and growth accelerates (Hasan, May, 2022).

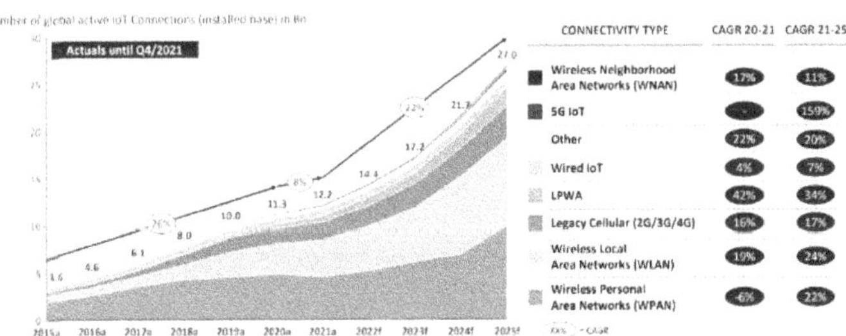

Fig: 3- *Number of global active IoT connections (Installed base) in billion (Hasan, May, 2022)*

As shown in fig.3, after the introduction of 5G technology in the market (2020) there is a huge expectation in the increase in active IoT devices globally. Fig.4 shows the expected market growth of IoT market globally ($M) and the selection of the IoT network operators which may play an important role in supply chain management 4.0.

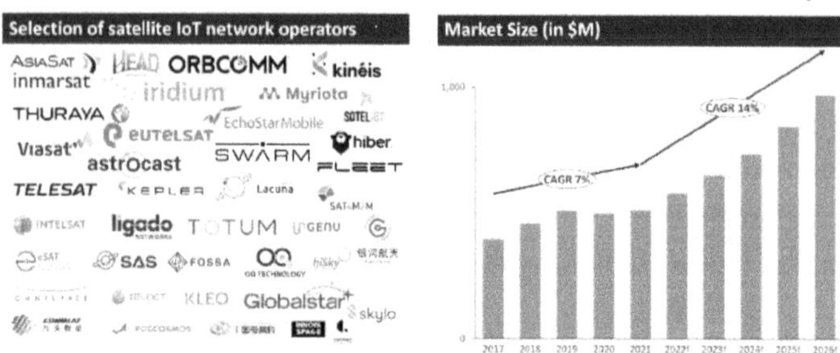

Fig: 4- The expected market size of IoT and network operators (Hasan, May, 2022)

5   Conclusion

The supply chain (SC) is essential for transporting goods across long distances and for fostering connections among various stakeholders, including producers, retailers, wholesalers, logistics providers, and customers. It is only possible by using the modern tooling system such as Artificial intelligence, IoT, machine learning, cloud computing, operational research and Data analytics. Our study fills a significant gap in the literature by demonstrating how various modern tools can be applied to supply chain management and how it enhances operational efficiency. Our study is distinctive because it examines various actual SCM improvements possibilities in the areas of customer management, production management, quality management, and services management in addition to summarizing the most recent data related with the active IoT devices which can play an important role in acquiring the data.

References

Ashton, K. (2009). That Internet of Things Thing. RFID Journal (2009). *URL: http://www. rfidjournal. com/articles/view, 4986.*

Choudhari, A., Rane, A., Talkar, S., Rayar, P., & Shukla, D. (2021). Designing and Prototyping for Conservation and Effective Utilization of Waste Heat from Air Conditioner. IOP Conference Series: Materials Science and Engineering,

Choudhari, A., Talkar, S., Rayar, P., & Rane, A. (2020). Design and Manufacturing of Compact and Portable Smart CNC Machine. Proceedings of International Conference on Intelligent Manufacturing and Automation,

de Vass, T., Shee, H., & Miah, S. J. (2021). IoT in supply chain management: Opportunities and challenges for businesses in early industry 4.0 context. *Operations and Supply Chain Management: An International Journal, 14*(2), 148-161.

Duan, Y., Edwards, J. S., & Dwivedi, Y. K. (2019). Artificial intelligence for decision making in the era of Big Data–evolution, challenges and research agenda. *International journal of information management, 48*, 63-71.

Dubey, R., Gunasekaran, A., Childe, S. J., Bryde, D. J., Giannakis, M., Foropon, C., . . . Hazen, B. T. (2020). Big data analytics and artificial intelligence pathway to operational performance under the effects of entrepreneurial orientation and environmental dynamism: A study of manufacturing organisations. *International Journal of Production Economics, 226*, 107599.

Dutta, P. K., & Mitra, S. (2021). Application of agricultural drones and IoT to understand food supply chain during post COVID-19. *Agricultural Informatics: Automation Using the IoT and Machine Learning*, 67-87.

Economic Indicators Division, R. I. B.-. (August 19, 2022). U.S Census Bureau News. In. Washington D.C: U.S Department of Commerce.

Evtodieva, T. E., Chernova, D. V., Ivanova, N. V., & Wirth, J. (2020). The internet of things: possibilities of application in intelligent supply chain management. *Digital transformation of the economy: Challenges, trends and new opportunities*, 395-403.

Gu, Y., & Jing, T. (2011). The IOT research in supply chain management of fresh agricultural products.

Gupta, A., Choudhari, A., Kadaka, T., & Rayar, P. (2019). Design and analysis of vertical vacuum fryer.

Hasan, M. (May, 2022). State of IoT 2022: Number of connected IoT devices growing 18% to 14.4 billion globally. In: IOT Analytics.

Hiromoto, R. E., Haney, M., & Vakanski, A. (2017). A secure architecture for IoT with supply chain risk management.

Lee, I., & Lee, K. (2015). The Internet of Things (IoT): Applications, investments, and challenges for enterprises. *Business horizons, 58*(4), 431-440.

Leung, Y. T., Cheng, F., Lee, Y. M., & Hennessy, J. J. (2007). A tool set for exploring the value of RFID in a supply chain. *Trends in supply chain design and management*, 49-70.

Mahroof, K. (2019). A human-centric perspective exploring the readiness towards smart warehousing: The case of a large retail distribution warehouse. *International Journal of Information Management, 45*, 176-190.

Manavalan, E., & Jayakrishna, K. (2019). A review of Internet of Things (IoT) embedded sustainable supply chain for industry 4.0 requirements. *Computers & Industrial Engineering, 127*, 925-953.

Seyedghorban, Z., Tahernejad, H., Meriton, R., & Graham, G. (2020). Supply chain digitalization: past, present and future. *Production Planning & Control, 31*(2-3), 96-114.

Talkar, S., Choudhari, A., & Rayar, P. (2020). Building Envelope Optimization and Cost-Effective Approach in HVAC to Support Smart Manufacturing. Proceedings of International Conference on Intelligent Manufacturing and Automation,

Tammela, I., Canen, A. G., & Helo, P. (2008). Time-based competition and multiculturalism: a comparative approach to the Brazilian, Danish and Finnish furniture industries. *Management Decision*.

Zahedi, A., Salehi-Amiri, A., Smith, N. R., & Hajiaghaei-Keshteli, M. (2021). Utilizing IoT to design a relief supply chain network for the SARS-COV-2 pandemic. *Applied Soft Computing, 104*, 107210.

Chapter 10
A Critical Review of Industry 4.0's Digital Transformation with New Trend Of Visual Brand Communication through Experiential Engagement

Sandhya Singh[1], Vinay Kandpal[2], Nusrat Zahan Nuzee[3]

[1]Rajiv Academy Technology & Management Mathura

[2]School of Business, University of Petroleum and Energy Studies, Dehradun

[3]Linkedin Influencer, Global Goodwill Ambassdor (Humanitarian) Bangladesh

Abstract:

In the information era, leveraging the power of the internet of things and knowledge elements, the customer comes to the purchasing table well prepared. The brands are challenged to upkeep the customer requirements and create delight. There is a lot of buzz on how content marketing can influence target customer groups. This chapter provides a perspective of the fuelling rise of visual communication strategies adopted by brands in creating experiential engagement. A glimpse into the cosmetic brands' digital engagement perspective is presented. There is presently a lack of content-focused research on the application of these Industry 4.0 cutting-edge technologies in environmentally friendly production. To clarify how these revolutionary technologies could affect the economic, social, and environmental aspects of the manufacturing industries, a thorough literature review was done.

Keywords- Industrial model 4.0, the Fourth Industrial Revolution, Internet of Things and. Cyber-physical systems (CPS) and Internet of services.

1. Introduction

Industry 4.0 describes a networked business ecosystem in which value chain participants link their infrastructure, machines, insights, and assets to form cyber-physical systems that can communicate and be controlled by one another decentralised and through the exchange of information that leads to decisions and actions.

Industry 4.0 marks the era of digitization and integration of digital technology and automation in business processes. Innovation is getting progressed and everything is getting accessible with the snap of the catch. Individuals are getting increasingly reliant on smartphones and the web. The ascent of online media started in the year 2004 when Facebook was introduced to the world. A 2020 report reveals that there are around 2.45 billion dynamic users every month. As the pandemic hit the utilization of web-based media saw a colossal ascent. In 2020 survey shows there was hype among 65-year age users and young people are utilizing Facebook as much as they utilized previously. Instagram has around 990 million users all across the globe. A normal human goes through around 3-4 hours via web-based media every day whether it's Facebook, Instagram, Snapchat or Tumblr. CPS collaborate and interact with people in real time via the Internet of Things (IOT). The value chain players provide and utilise internal and cross-organizational services via the Internet of Services (IOS).

Literature Review
Industry 4.0

The fourth industrial revolution is only being started right now. The fourth industrial revolution is being advanced by advances in digital technologies like artificial intelligence, robots, 3D printing, the IoT, along with nano- and bio-technology and material sciences. Industry 4.0 technologies will have a significant influence on all fields of study, redrawing the borders between the commercial and industrial sectors as well as between buyers and sellers, altering the function of the public and private sectors, and altering the rules of competition.

The Main Pillars of Industrial 4.0

- **IOT**
- **CPS**
- **IOS**

IOT (The Industrial Internet of Things (IoT)-

The Internet of Things (IoT) is the next technology revolution that will rely on cloud-based systems to provide compute, analytics, and other solutions. IOT's primary goal is to link the Internet by gathering data from real-world things. Computers or other advanced gadgets make operational decisions by gathering data (Rahman and Rahmani, 2017). The Industrial Internet combines the Internet's widespread accessibility with a brand-new capability to directly manage the physical environment, including equipment, buildings, and infrastructure. connected by software platforms will better facilitate data creation, aggregation, and sharing.

CPS (Cyber-physical systems)-

Cyber-physical systems (CPS) are designed systems that rely on the fusion of physical elements and computing methods. Cyber-physical systems are created by combining embedded systems with the internet, online data, and services. The way humans engage with engineered systems will change thanks to CPS, which are enabling technologies.

(IOS) Internet of Services

Products, operations, and services being "refined" in industry more and more by being integrated to create smart services. Internet-based services have a lot of potential for development, both for IT service providers and customers. These services, for instance, may result in alterations to product portfolios, improvements to industrial plant management via new knowledge platforms, and virtualization of ICT infrastructures with appropriate consideration of related IT security risks.

Narrating the Brand story visually

Visual communication alludes to the act of addressing an idea or thought in an infographic, picture, video and sketch structure which can impart the plans to the crowd in a straightforward yet emotional manner. In the current time of online media, visual communications are considered a vital fix in brand communication. The web-based media clients vigorously rely upon the visual substance to impart. This should be possible by recounting stories, engaging their companions or by offering their feelings to other people. Visual communication is a significant method to improve customer engagement, readership and deals.

Within excess of 3 billion pictures shared every day, online organizations are putting forth a valiant effort to make important visual substance to pull in a more extensive crowd. They are additionally embracing better procedures to settle on better business and advertising choices to identify, comprehend and follow up on all the pictures that are pertinent to their brands. Advertisers who grasp visual substance acquire more significant yields, for example, comments, likes, shares, visits and saves.

Visual communication can be extensively classified in the accompanying classification which is-

• **Stylist Image** – This incorporates the static drawing, picture or as of late the stylish image. The representations are short in nature and extremely appealing.

• **Comics-** the assortments of pictures and text adjust to frame a storyline. This kind of visual substance incorporates infographics and visual stories.

• **Videos-** the assortment of moving pictures with an unmistakable story or exhibit. Video exhibits and brings greater engagement. It very well may be in a type of instructional exercise or story.

This permits supporters to communicate their perspectives through digital engagement.

Fostering Customer Digital Engagement

Customer advanced engagement alludes to an organization's endeavours to assemble associations with people through customized cooperation on computerized channels, to acquire and hold steadfast clients.

Effective consumer engagement achieves that objective by:

• **Distinguishing the brand from its rivals-**Customer engagement is turning into a significant piece of brand communication as it carries a preferred position to both the brand just as the customer

• **High web-based media engagement prompting Brand prominence-** This additionally fortifies the customer-brand relationship. The restorative industry utilizes a high calibre of visual substances like pictures, video and images.

Visual communication is astoundingly effective at evoking thought, hastening intuitive responses, and influencing emotions, ultimately leading to a shift in attitudes about the brand. But because so many individuals and organizations put their content online, there is a huge amount of information.

Consumer engagement and visual content in advertising have long been linked, and this relationship has only accelerated with the spread of technological advances in internet media.

Visual content classification

Client engagement refers to the passionate attachment between a customer and a brand, which depends on the extent of the customer's involvement in the purchase of the goods, participation on social media, association of the customers with the brand, and influence over time.

It is obvious that images influence consumer engagement, but it is still unclear whether types of visual content are effective at capturing the attention of online media clients.

Visual content has been divided into three categories- Informational content, Engaging content, and Incentive content.

- **Informational Content-** The buyer will believe that this particular brand is significant or agreeable as a result of this kind of content. As they are more appealing, engaging, and simple to comprehend and will typically receive more likes, tweets, and retweets, other media, such as videos, slideshows, diagrams, graphs, and infographics, can be used to consolidate the data and present it to web-based media clients.

- **Engaging Content-** The significant persuasive components for consumer support rely on the consumer's advantage to encounter engaging content in the brand post. The consumer will appreciate the content and attempt to like the offer or remark and increment the engagement.

- **Incentive Content**- Compensation is something that spurs a person to play out an activity. Individuals who are affected by the compensation will in general join brand gatherings, online networks and brand pages on various social networking sites and remark on pictures, recordings, and also reproduce the posts.

2. A Glimpse into the Visual Brand Communication strategies adopted by cosmetic brands

Strong brands provide customers purpose and value. These are crucial factors to take into account for luxury businesses since they rely on customers who place a high value on their products. things and are willing to pay a higher price (Hutton) In order to create a brand identity, businesses should offer advertisement messages that interact with consumers the originality and personality of the brand, and most recently,

The use of social media for such advertising has increased (Hussain & Nandan 2005; Ferdous 2014). Using visual brand identity is one way to communicate brand identity. contact points These visual signals for sensory perception include Taglines, phrases, and colours that provide customers having distinctive brand connections. These sensory-visual clues have demonstrated the ability to distinguish items, permit businesses to charge premium pricing, and bestow competitive

While visual brand communication strategies are being used across sectors, for the beauty and cosmetics industry marketing campaigns with visual content have become a signature technique with neuro-creative research in vogue today. The nation's beauty care products and cosmetics market is relied upon to enrol yearly development of 25 per cent contacting USD 20 billion by 2025. The Indian cosmetics and makeup industry make up USD 6.5 billion from a worldwide market of USD 274 billion. It is worth getting a glimpse into customer digital engagement practices with the cosmetics brand pages. Instagram and Facebook are the most popular social media platforms where users engage with brands, with the largest volume of engagement attributed to video content and images. Users are seen liking, sharing reposting the content, peer recommendations etc., however, the conversion does not happen with mere engagement. This involves business along with involvement, expectation, and emotion. Mission and client involvement are combined in this.

Social media has grown in importance as a platform for businesses to advertise their goods. A trend of designing items to fit a social media aware lifestyle has emerged, and in addition to Facebook and Twitter, rising platforms like Instagram and YouTube have altered the trajectory of the brand market and consumer buying

According to Haenlein & Kaplan (2010:61), "Social Media is a series of Internet-based applications that build on the ideological and technological underpinnings of Web 2.0, and that allow the creation and exchange of User Generated Content," is the term used to describe social media. The comment effectively demonstrates how social media differs from traditional online material in that people both consume and produce the information on these sites. Social media use has integrated naturally into daily life, making it simpler than ever to connect and communicate with friends, family, and businesses.

Borrowed from Roberts's (2005) three storytelling elements (myths, iconic characters, and dreams), Cho and his colleagues used mystery to represent cognitive dimension of a brand image "shaped by great stories, past and present interactions with a brand, as well as future dreams and aspirations reflecting a certain lifestyle" and developed four primary themes of mystery:

(a) Positive present experiences;

(b) Positive memories from past experience,

(c) Future aspirations, and

(d) Self-congruity.

3. The Road Ahead

The Metaverse is quickly evolving into a new playground for companies as its adoption spreads across industries. The options are endless in the metaverse, from selecting a virtual automobile test drive to purchasing and donning digital clothing for one's avatars. Digital avatars that are powered by conversational AI and have the cutting-edge ability to communicate like humans would be used by brands to assist their customers as they buy in the metaverse

Due to the fact that every business, regardless of size, is trying to increase efficiency, digital has emerged as the foundation of the manufacturing industry. Every firm must now win the war on cost cutting since the present economy is putting pressure on revenue growth. These platforms have developed over the past ten years to now include social networking sites like Facebook, photo and video sharing websites like Instagram and YouTube, business networking websites like LinkedIn, microblogging services like Twitter, and wiki sites (e.g., Wikipedia: Dawley 2009; Mangold and Faulds 2009). The fastest-growing social media platforms include photo-sharing websites like Instagram, Pinterest, and Snapchat (McNely 2012).

4. Discussion

Industry 4.0 describes a networked business ecosystem in which value chain participants link their infrastructure, machines, insights, and assets to form cyber-physical systems that can communicate and be controlled by one another decentralised and through the exchange of information that leads to decisions and actions.

. It is easier to quickly manage a visual sign than it is to read through each sentence of a lengthy text section. One picture may communicate a thousand words therefore a picture can convey a lot of information quickly. Visual communication improves the clearness of data. The fundamental explanation lies in the psychological capacity of the human cerebrum. Since the bigger measure of data is accessible via online media, the clients like to skirt a huge number until they discover them more alluring and are persuaded that it is valuable to them. Strong brands provide customers purpose and value. Instagram and Facebook are the most popular social media platforms where users engage with brands, with the largest volume of engagement attributed to video content and images. Users are seen liking, sharing reposting the content, peer recommendations etc., however, the conversion does not happen with mere engagement.

5. Conclusion

Industry 4.0 is the current concept that will use CPS to develop new business models and shape the future of several sectors. Investigating its dimensions is essential in order to achieve efficiency in the corporate environment. The ideas of Industry 4.0 are briefly discussed in this essay, along with how they might assist businesses in achieving their Industry 4.0 goals. Following a review of the literature, the BCG's findings regarding Industry 4.0 are used to define Industry 4.0's some pillars: IOT, CPS, IOS. The study starts out by giving a summary of the body of existing academic research on the application of these cutting-edge technologies. in green manufacturing. The essay then categorises the function of these creative technology to the industrial supply chain's sustainable performance. Industry 4.0 is still in its infancy for the majority of businesses, and the digital transformation will need strong leadership, the appropriate human competencies, and to get over the numerous obstacles that have been identified as impeding its successful implementation.

References

Akhtar, P. et al. (2017). The Internet of Things, dynamic data and information processing capabilities, and operational agility. *Technological Forecasting and Social Change*. Available at: http://linkinghub.elsevier.com/retrieve/pii/S0040162517305504.

ATZORI, Luigi. Antonio, Iera. and Giacomo, Morabito. (2010). *"The internet of things: A survey."* Computer networks 54.15. 2787-2805.

Bennett, D. R. & Kunze, C. (2016, September). Is a visual worth more than a thousand words? An investigation into brand engagement and social shopping on visual social media. *In XXIV AEDEM International Conference*.

BRETTEL, Malte, et al. (2014). "How virtualization, decentralization and network building change the manufacturing landscape: An Industry 4.0 Perspective." *International Journal of Science, Engineering and Technology* 8 (1), 37- 44.

Brodie, R. J, Ilic, A., Juric, B., & Hollebeek, L. (2013). Consumer engagement in a virtual brand community: An exploratory analysis. *Journal of business research*, 66(1), 105-114.

Bucherer, E., Eisert, U. and Gassmann, G. (2012). Towards systematic business model innovation: Lessons from product innovation management. *Creativity and Innovation Management,* 21(2), 183–198.

Cheah, J. H., Ting, H., Cham, T. H., & Memon, M. A. (2019). The effect of selfie promotion and celebrity endorsed advertisement on decision-making processes: *A model comparison. Internet Research,* 29(3), 552-577.

Clairand, J.-M.; Briceno-Leon, M.; Escriva-Escriva, G.; Pantaleo, A.M. (2020) .Review of Energy Efficiency Technologies in the Food Industry: *Trends, Barriers, and Opportunities. IEEE Access*, 8, 48015–48029.

Gizem Erboz.(2017). How to Define Industry 4.0: The Main Pillars Of Industry 4.0 on Managerial trends in the development of enterprises in globalization era. At: *Slovak University of Agriculture in Nitra, Slovakia.*

Hermann, M., Pentek, T. and Otto, B. (2016). Design principles for Industry 4.0 scenarios, in: 2016 49th *Hawaii International Conference on System Sciences (HICSS), IEEE, 3928–3937*

Khan, S., Ali, S. and Singh, R. (2022). Determinants of Remanufacturing Adoption for Circular Economy: A Causal Relationship Evaluation Framework, *Applied System Innovation,* 5(4), 62. https://doi.org/10.3390/asi5040062.

Khan, S., Singh, R. and Kirti. (2021). Critical Factors for Blockchain Technology Implementation: A Supply Chain Perspective, *Journal of Industrial Integration and Management,* 2150011.
https://doi.org/10.1142/s2424862221500111.

Khan, S., Singh, R., Haleem, A., Dsilva, J. and Ali, S. (2022). Exploration of Critical Success Factors of Logistics 4.0: A DEMATEL Approach, *Logistics,* 6(1), 13.
https://doi.org/10.3390/logistics6010013.

Kujur, F, & Singh, S. (2020) . Visual communication and consumer-brand relationship on social networking sites-uses &

gratifications theory perspective. *Journal of theoretical and applied electronic commerce research,* 15(1).

Lexington, MA. Lexington Book. Muehling, D.D., and M. McCann. (1993) .Attitude toward the ad: A review. *Journal of Current Issues and Research in Advertising* 15(1): 25–58.

M.V., A.V. Hooft, and U. Nederstigt. (2014). Finding the tipping point: Visual metaphor and conceptual complexity in advertising. *Journal of Advertising* 43(4): 333–343.

Manic, M. (2015) Marketing engagement through visual content. *Bulletin of the Transilvania University of Brasov. Economic Sciences.* Series V, 8(2), 89.

McBride-Chang, C., Lin, D., Liu, P. D., Aram, D., Levin, I., Cho, J.-R., Shu, H., & Zhang, Y. (2012). The ABC's of Chinese: Maternal mediation of Pinyin for Chinese children's early literacy skills. *Reading and Writing,* 25(1), 283–300. https://doi.org/10.1007/s11145-010-9270.

Monroe, K.B., and R. Krishnan. (1985). The effect of price on subjective product evaluation. In The perception of merchandise and store quality, ed. J. Jacoby and J. Olson, 209–232.

Nandan, S. (2005). An exploration of the brand identity–brand image linkage: A communications perspective. *Journal of Brand Management* 12(4): 264–278.

Negm, E., & Tantawi, P. (2015). Investigating the impact of visual design on consumers' perceptions towards advertising. *International Journal of Scientific and Research Publications,* 5(4), 1-9.

Nunes, P.F., B.A. Johnson, and R.T. Breene. (2004). Selling to the moneyed masses. *Harvard Business Review* 82: 94–104.

Pachar, S., Singh, R. and Wahid, M. (2021). Implication of Renewable Energy in Sustainable Development in India: Future

Strategy, *IOP Conference Series: Material Science and Engineering,* 1149(1), 012020. https://doi.org/10.1088/1757-899x/1149/1/012020.

Pachar, S., Singh, R.(2021). Role of Sustainable development goals and corporate social responsibility in India's growth: opportunities and challenges, *Empirical Economics Letters,* 20(2), 277-281.

R, Amit.& Zott, C. (2012). Creating value through business model *innovation MIT Sloan Management Review,* 53(3), 41-49.

Singh, R et al. (2022). Quality 4.0 in Healthcare: Application of the EFQM Excellence Mode. *Empirical Economics Letters,* 21(2), 1-19.

Singh, R. (2018). The Cause of Unemployment in Current Market Scenario, *Vivechan International Journal of Research,* 9(1), 86-81.

Singh, R., DSilva, J. and Kumar, R. S. (2021). Modelling the CSR Initiatives on Firm Performance: A Context of Emerging Economies, *Empirical Economic Letters,* 20 (3), 221-228.

Singh, R., Dsilva, J., Centobelli, P. and Tripathi, V. (2021). A review on Sustainable HRM: A study evaluating Sustainability for organisational development, The Empirical Economics Letters, 20(2), 1-10.

Singh, R., Khan, S. and Dsilva, J. (2022). A framework for assessment of critical factor for circular economy practice implementation, *Journal of Modelling in Management,* https://doi.org/10.1108/jm2-06-2021-0145.

Singh, S, Singh, R, Shandilya, T and Kumar, R.S. (2021). Digital security issues in emerging technology management, *Empirical Economics Letters,* 20(5), 205-213.

Chapter 11
Innovative Human Resource Practices: Role of Blockchain Technology

Swati Agrawal

School of Management, Bennett University, Greater Noida

Abstract

Technological modernization has completely revolutionized data and business management practices in present times. This article tends to examine the adoption of technologies like blockchain in the area of human resource management (HRM) of organizations. The current study explores a unique set of factors selected from the extensive literature and acquired information from experts having significant experience of blockchain technology in their respective organizations. Blockchain technology enhance the employee learning records and update the real-time information in HR database technologies.

Keywords: Blockchain, Human Resource, HR Efficiency, Technology in HR

1. Introduction

Blockchain technology is considered an extensive innovative synergist revolutionizing the structure of interaction, creation or valuation between businesses, customers, societies, partners, and individuals (Hughes, L et al., 2019). Blockchain was initially determined by Santoshi Nakamoto as the world's first decentralized digital currency managing technique (Nakamoto S.,2008). Bitcoin network was developed with blockchain technology as its underlying infrastructure (Beck, R. 2018). Blockchain is an architecture based on peer-to-peer (p2p) networking that stores the transactions in the structure of blocks and each of them is chained to the former block using cryptographic assurance systems (Kabra, N et al.,2020; Alsunaidi, S et al.,2019).

According to the world economic forum predictive analysis, 10% of the global GDP would be on hybrid blockchain technologies by 2025. Blockchain is an emerging technology that add significant value in the HR domain and streamlines various activities of HR professionals. Human resource departments, being the most integral component of the organizations entangled with coordinating substantial tasks varying from recruiting and retaining the best talent, processing payroll, regulatory compliance reporting, providing a safe working environment, activating training & development programs and offering incentives to achieve organizational objectives (Stone, D. L et al., 2015). Blockchain-based applications will proliferate innovative platforms for HR professionals with immense benefits, thus shifting their conventional operational role to a more strategic role. Blockchain networks can serve as an imperative instrument for the verification of individual identities, educational background checks, and employment histories, thus leading to attract quality talent for the job position (Liu, L et al.,2020). This will enable the HR recruiters to verify the employee credentials, strength, weakness and gives comprehensive based records to make a better decision (Wang, X et. al.,2017). The automated process driven blockchain technology will reduce manual work while allowing managers to immerse themselves in more value-adding activities such as employee experience and engagement. Additionally, blockchain tech has the potential to provide real-time verification of cross border payments, without the need for intermediaries such as banks, third party and clearinghouses, thus workers can be paid instantly with the use of smart contracts (Secinaro, S.et al.,2021; Pan, X et al.,2020). There is also a possibility that the performance appraisal model associated with rewards, recognition and salary increments can be re-designed with the distributed ledger platform in organizations (Mahyuni, L. P et al. 2020; Bai, C et al.2020).

2.   Blockchain application and its Characteristics

Blockchain technology is one of the most secure and advanced form of technological innovation across industries, practitioners and academia. Blockchain technology has versatile uses apart from recording financial transactions (Liebenau, J et al.,2016). Blockchain can be utilized for asset tracking and registration, decentralized voting and governance, healthcare information and much more (Albayati, H et al.,2020; McGhin, T et al.,2019). Blockchain can be defined as a fully distributed and decentralized database that stores a congruent, immutable and chronological log of transactions between network participants (Mansfield-Devine, S et al., 2017). The record of validated information gets sealed by a cryptographic algorithm, linking blocks of data in form of a chain to ensure data integrity and standardized arrangement for the data access (Tang, H et al.,2019). Each block contains the encrypted data and reference links to the preceding block hence maximizing the data preservation with a coded security system.

3.   Blockchain technology in human resource management Practices

Blockchain is cultivating momentous excitement in many aspects of industries by virtue of its design and architecture. Sivathanu (2019) demonstrated that blockchain technology has great potential to upend HR functions that are not just restricted to talent management such as recruiting, developing and retaining new-age talent for achieving high-performance at an organizational level.

Blockchain will deeply impact HR responsibilities, thus going to disrupt big picture areas like hiring, payroll with its impressive services (Frizzo-Barker et al.,2020).Due to lack of skilled workers and talent wars, one of the most prominent adoption waves of blockchain may lie in hiring process. The hiring process has become a daunting task for the human resource department of the organizations due to the false information provided by the job applicants on their CVs. The disruptive blockchain technology reduces the occurrence of unscrupulous entries and employers before hiring a candidate can get their most precise delineation and contestant's credentials. Thus, the integration of blockchain will verify the data submitted by the employee will provide genuine, transparent information, reduce costs and make it more effective (Chen, Y. C et al.,2019). Blockchain technology has the prospective to eradicate exaggeration in the case of resume screening. Upon successfully verifying the candidate data, organizations can quickly release the offer letter, thereby saving significant time, effort and cost in the recruitment process (Ghazali, O et al.,2018). Concurrently, individuals can enhance their employability by voluntarily sharing their data with the recruiters as it improves employment opportunities and creates a culture of trust between the employee and the employers. Moreover, technology can be utilized to gather the employee training and development records to be stored in the database (Lam, T. Y., & Dongol, B. et al., 2020). The growing fast paced technological advancement and transparency in the organizational system has also proposed the blockchain-enabled training effectiveness measurement (BETEM) model for imparting and evaluating training exercises for their employees. Blockchain will ease HR professionals' roles through its secure data-sharing feature to verify and evaluate the education and the skills of the recruits. Therefore, first outbreak will open door to authenticate candidate sourcing along with their resume verification and background screening, thus full disclosure of their employment histories. Blockchain may automate the victorious moments such as tittle changes or promotion as well as unsatisfactory performance reviews or reason for layoff before candidates are presented to hiring professionals. That means recruiters can access the information about each candidate in real time rather than receiving traditional resumes or viewing career networking websites like LinkedIn in near future. Thus, recruiters can direct the right candidate to the well-suited role in organization with blockchain new hiring game plan.

Blockchain technology also emerged as potential disruptor in payment solutions arena. The greatest challenges faced by HR department in maintaining high volume financial operations. The procedure that employees values the most such as payroll process, taxes, cross border transactions, managing regulatory compliance can be made more faster, secure and transparent with the advent of blockchain in the gig economy(Bertino, E et al., 2019).The application of blockchain in payments system ensures that participating parties can share sensitive information in verified manner without relying on central authorities or third party intermediary, thus eliminating human errors and developing trusted network(Narayanaswami, C et., 2019). Moreover, decentralized payment services are also creating new roadmap that removes the unnecessary frictions associated with cross border payment (Gomber et al.,2018). In nutshell, HR managers would not be required to run a monthly payment or contact their company's bank, thus ensuring quick and low transmission cost for its customers or regulators. Instead, open real-time blockchain ledgers will help HR with invoice tracking as well as transaction distribution, invoicing, and reporting. Employees also don't have to wait for your payroll to be processed. Blockchain technology enables the development of more decentralized, innovative, interoperable, borderless, and transparent payment services.

The next big space where blockchain can be used to automate the performance evaluation system. The performance management cycle is crucial for all employees in an organization because it is associated with recognition, salary increases, training and career growth. With the introduction of online training courses, the availability of digital badges, and the vast array of courses, education and academic achievements, HR teams are finding it more difficult to maintain track of each employee's day-to-day activities in the organization (Nurhasanah, Y et al.,2020). Therefore, HR professionals are looking for new solutions to keep employees engaged and productive. The application or programme can be developed to create decentralized performance appraisal system using blockchain, smart contracts and crypto coins, thus providing a rewarding experience for an overall contribution of employees towards the organization over a given interval of time (Sifah et al., 2020)). As a result, an attempt is being made to use various technique and strategies that will encourage, engage, and create a high-performing talent pool in order to strengthen their skill set in the workplace (Prager, F et al., 2021).

4. Conclusion

Industry 4.0 is a paradigm that is transforming the way organization operate by utilizing cutting-edge technology. Blockchain is one of these technologies that can improve Industry 4.0 applications by ensuring protection, credibility, immutability, decentralization, and a greater level of automation via smart contracts. The application of blockchain technology in Industry 4.0 is estimated to rise and benefit a wide range of sectors and will further enhance and optimize various HR sectors to thrive in a competitive edge in this digitization era. Although blockchain has yet to be standardized in HR, it would be capable of determining smart solutions for verifying and simplifying the hiring process.

References

Hughes, L., Dwivedi, Y. K., Misra, S. K., Rana, N. P., Raghavan, V., & Akella, V. (2019). Blockchain research, practice and policy: Applications, benefits, limitations, emerging research themes and research agenda. International Journal of Information Management, 49, 114-129.

Nakamoto, S. (2008). Bitcoin: A peer-to-peer electronic cash system. Decentralized Business Review, 21260.

Beck, R. (2018). Beyond bitcoin: The rise of blockchain world. Computer, 51(2), 54-58

Casino, F., Dasaklis, T. K., & Patsakis, C. (2019). A systematic literature review of blockchain-based applications: Current status, classification and open issues. Telematics and informatics, 36, 55-81

Kabra, N., Bhattacharya, P., Tanwar, S., & Tyagi, S. (2020). MudraChain: Blockchain-based framework for automated cheque clearance in financial institutions. Future Generation Computer Systems, 102, 574-587

Alsunaidi, S. J., & Alhaidari, F. A. (2019, April). A survey of consensus algorithms for blockchain technology. In 2019 International Conference on Computer and Information Sciences (ICCIS) (pp. 1-6). IEEE.

Gartner (2020), "Blockchain technology: what's ahead?", available at: www.gartner.com/en/ information-technology/insights/blockchain

Hooper, A., & Holtbrügge, D. (2020). Blockchain technology in international business: changing the agenda for global governance. Review of International Business and Strategy.

Ingold, P. V., & Langer, M. (2021). Resume= Resume? The effects of blockchain, social media, and classical resumes on resume fraud and applicant reactions to resumes. Computers in Human Behavior, 114, 106573.

Arenas, R., & Fernandez, P. (2018, June). CredenceLedger: A permissioned blockchain for verifiable academic credentials. In 2018 IEEE International Conference on Engineering, Technology and Innovation (ICE/ITMC) (pp. 1-6). IEEE.

Stone, D. L., Deadrick, D. L., Lukaszewski, K. M., & Johnson, R. (2015). The influence of technology on the future of human resource management. Human resource management review, 25(2), 216-231.

Wang, X., Feng, L., Zhang, H., Lyu, C., Wang, L., & You, Y. (2017, April). Human resource information management model based on blockchain technology. In 2017 IEEE symposium on service-oriented system engineering (SOSE) (pp. 168-173). IEEE.

Secinaro, S., Calandra, D., & Biancone, P. (2021). Blockchain, trust, and trust accounting: can blockchain technology substitute trust created by intermediaries in trust accounting? A theoretical examination. International Journal of Management Practice, 14(2), 129-145.

Pan, X., Pan, X., Song, M., Ai, B., & Ming, Y. (2020). Blockchain technology and enterprise operational capabilities: An empirical test. International Journal of Information Management, 52, 101946.

Mahyuni, L. P. et al., (2020). Mapping the potentials of blockchain in improving supply chain performance. Cogent Business & Management, 7(1), 1788329.

Bai, C., & Sarkis, J. (2020). A supply chain transparency and sustainability technology appraisal model for blockchain technology. International Journal of Production Research, 58(7), 2142-2162

Hong, S. J., & Tam, K. Y. (2006). Understanding the adoption of multipurpose information appliances: The case of mobile data services. Information systems research, 17(2), 162-179.

Folkinshteyn, D., & Lennon, M. (2016). Braving Bitcoin: A technology acceptance model (TAM) analysis. Journal of Information Technology Case and Application Research, 18(4), 220-249.

Williams, M. D., Rana, N. P., & Dwivedi, Y. K. (2015). The unified theory of acceptance and use of technology (UTAUT): a literature review. Journal of enterprise information management.

Chang, C. M., Liu, L. W., Huang, H. C., & Hsieh, H. H. (2019). Factors influencing online hotel booking: Extending UTAUT2 with age, gender, and experience as moderators. Information, 10(9), 281.

Morosan, C., & DeFranco, A. (2016). It's about time: Revisiting UTAUT2 to examine consumers' intentions to use NFC mobile payments in hotels. International Journal of Hospitality Management, 53, 17-29.

Venkatesh, V., Thong, J. Y., & Xu, X. (2012). Consumer acceptance and use of information technology: extending the unified theory of acceptance and use of technology. MIS quarterly, 157-178.

Albayati, H., Kim, S. K., & Rho, J. J. (2020). Accepting financial transactions using blockchain technology and cryptocurrency: A customer perspective approach. *Technology in Society*, *62*, 101320.

McGhin, T., Choo, K. K. R., Liu, C. Z., & He, D. (2019). Blockchain in healthcare applications: Research challenges and opportunities. *Journal of Network and Computer Applications*, *135*, 62-75.

Mansfield-Devine, S. (2017). Beyond Bitcoin: using blockchain technology to provide assurance in the commercial world. *Computer Fraud & Security*, *2017*(5), 14-18.

Xie, J., Tang, H., Huang, T., Yu, F. R., Xie, R., Liu, J., & Liu, Y. (2019). A survey of blockchain technology applied to smart cities: Research issues and challenges. *IEEE Communications Surveys & Tutorials*, *21*(3), 2794-2830.

Tönnissen, S., & Teuteberg, F. (2020). Analysing the impact of blockchain-technology for operations and supply chain management: An explanatory model drawn from multiple case studies. *International Journal of Information Management*, *52*, 101953.

Howson, P. (2020). Building trust and equity in marine conservation and fisheries supply chain management with blockchain. *Marine Policy*, *115*, 103873.

Çaldağ, M. T., & Gökalp, E. (2020). Exploring Critical success factors for blockchain-based intelligent transportation systems. *Emerg. Sci. J*, *4*, 27-44.

Ahmad, R. W., Hasan, H., Jayaraman, R., Salah, K., & Omar, M. (2021). Blockchain applications and architectures for port operations and logistics management. *Research in Transportation Business & Management*, 100620.

Kamble, S. S., Gunasekaran, A., & Sharma, R. (2020). Modeling the blockchain enabled traceability in agriculture supply chain. *International Journal of Information Management, 52*, 101967.

Tanwar, S., Parekh, K., & Evans, R. (2020). Blockchain-based electronic healthcare record system for healthcare 4.0 applications. *Journal of Information Security and Applications, 50*, 102407.

Li, Z., Bahramirad, S., Paaso, A., Yan, M., & Shahidehpour, M. (2019). Blockchain for decentralized transactive energy management system in networked microgrids. *The Electricity Journal, 32*(4), 58-72.

White, G. R. (2017). Future applications of blockchain in business and management: A Delphi study. *Strategic Change, 26*(5), 439-451.

Onik, M. M. H., Aich, S., Yang, J., Kim, C. S., & Kim, H. C. (2019). Blockchain in healthcare: Challenges and solutions. In *Big data analytics for intelligent healthcare management* (pp. 197-226). Academic Press.

Sivathanu, B., & Pillai, R. (2019). Technology and talent analytics for talent management–a game changer for organizational performance. International Journal of Organizational Analysis

Frizzo-Barker, J., Chow-White, P. A., Adams, P. R., Mentanko, J., Ha, D., & Green, S. (2020). Blockchain as a disruptive technology for business: A systematic review. International Journal of Information Management, 51, 102029

Ghazali, O., & Saleh, O. S. (2018). A graduation certificate verification model via utilization of the blockchain technology. Journal of Telecommunication, Electronic and Computer Engineering (JTEC), 10(3-2), 29-34.

Lam, T. Y., & Dongol, B. (2020). A blockchain-enabled e-learning platform. Interactive Learning Environments, 1-23.

Bertino, E., Kundu, A., & Sura, Z. (2019). Data transparency with blockchain and AI ethics. *Journal of Data and Information Quality (JDIQ)*, *11*(4), 1-8.

Narayanaswami, C., Nooyi, R., Govindaswamy, S. R., & Viswanathan, R. (2019). Blockchain anchored supply chain automation. *IBM Journal of Research and Development*, *63*(2/3), 7-1.

Gomber, P., Kauffman, R. J., Parker, C., & Weber, B. W. (2018). On the fintech revolution: Interpreting the forces of innovation, disruption, and transformation in financial services. Journal of management information systems, 35(1), 220-265.

Nurhasanah, Y., Prameswari, D., & Fachrunnisa, O. (2020, April). Blockchain-Based Solution for Effective Employee Management. In International conference on smart computing and cyber security: strategic foresight, security challenges and innovation (pp. 147-154). Springer, Singapore.

Sifah, E. B., Xia, H., Cobblah, C. N. A., Xia, Q., Gao, J., & Du, X. (2020). BEMPAS: a decentralized employee performance assessment system based on blockchain for smart city governance. IEEE Access, 8, 99528-99539

Prager, F., Martinez, J., & Cagle, C. (2021). Blockchain and Regional Workforce Development: Identifying Opportunities and Training Needs. In Blockchain and the Public Sector (pp. 47-72). Springer, Cham.Review, 93(4), 40-50.

Velasquez, M., & Hester, P. T. (2013). An analysis of multi-criteria decision making methods. International journal of operations research, 10(2), 56-66.

Le, T. P. N., Genovese, A., & Koh, L. S. (2012). Using FAHP to determine the criteria for partner's selection within a green supply chain: The case of hand tool industry in Taiwan. Journal of Manufacturing Technology Management.

Chauhan, A., Singh, A., & Jharkharia, S. (2018). An interpretive structural modeling (ISM) and decision-making trail and evaluation laboratory (DEMATEL) method approach for the analysis of barriers of waste recycling in India. Journal of the Air & Waste Management Association, 68(2), 100-110.

Heo, M., Kim, N., & Faith, M. S. (2015). Statistical power as a function of Cronbach alpha of instrument questionnaire items. BMC medical research methodology, 15(1), 1-9.

Bonett, D. G., & Wright, T. A. (2015). Cronbach's alpha reliability: Interval estimation, hypothesis testing, and sample size planning. Journal of organizational behavior, 36(1), 3-15.

Lan, S., Zhang, H., Zhong, R. Y., & Huang, G. Q. (2016). A customer satisfaction evaluation model for logistics services using fuzzy analytic hierarchy process. Industrial Management & Data Systems.

Chapter 12
Industry 4.0 Paradigm– A future of marketing built on intelligent customer management systems, developing technologies, and operational excellence.

Mrinalini Choudhary

College of Business, Royal University for Women, Bahrain

Abstract

The objectives of this chapter is to assess the Industry 4.0 framework, define the Industry 4.0 paradigm, identify its drivers, discuss its possible effects, and identify its barriers. According to the study's findings, Industry 4.0 defines a future production system's vision; it is an unavoidable revolution and drastic shift that affects all industries and a wide variety of cutting-edge technology. Organizations can benefit greatly from Industry 4.0, which includes real-time data analysis, improved visibility, autonomous monitoring, better production, and competitiveness. Modern technologies are driving the Fourth Industrial Revolution, often known as Industry 4.0, which is having a huge impact on business structures and manufacturing procedures. During this revolution, new disruptive behaviors and technology have been introduced. These aspects of Industry 4.0 have a significant impact on marketing.

Over the next 10 years, many companies will probably be replaced due to new digital disruptors and the inability of existing repositioning businesses. Modern digital technologies are offering innovative opportunities for growth and innovation at all phases of the consumer journey. The emergence of

Industry 4.0 has made it possible for this digitally-driven evolution to take place.

Keywords: Industrial revolutions, Industry 4.0 drivers, Digital Transformation, Marketing challenges

1. Introduction

As a result of technological advancements and inventions, the global industrial environment has seen a remarkable transformation in recent years. The three previous industrial revolutions can be likened to Industry 4.0, which represents the biggest disruptive changes in the industry because of technological breakthroughs.

The First Industrial Revolution, which got started in Britain in the middle of the 18th century, was hastened by the invention of the steam engine. Midway through the nineteenth century.

The Second Industrial Revolution began to take place in both Europe and the United States. Mass production and the substitution of chemical and electrical energy for steam were the two main characteristics of this revolution. To satisfy the growing demand, a variety of technologies and automation were created, which enhanced productivity. The development of the integrated circuit served as the catalyst for the Third Industrial Revolution (microchip). This revolution, which began in many industrialized nations around the world in the latter years of the 20th century, is notable for using electronics and information technology to achieve increased automation in manufacturing as per *Deloitte AG. Industry 4.0*.

The goal of every industrial revolution has been to increase productivity. With the help of cutting-edge technological innovations like steam engines, electricity, and digital technology, the first three industrial revolutions had a profound impact on industrial operations. The fourth industrial revolution, often known as Industry 4.0, is a highly complicated framework that has been widely discussed and explored. It significantly affects the industrial sector because it brings about advances that are pertinent to smart and futuristic manufacturing. This emerging idea of Industry 4.0 is a catch-all name for a new industrial paradigm that encompasses technologies like Robotics, Big Data, Cloud Manufacturing, Augmented Reality, and Cyber-Physical Systems.

2. Industry Overview
2.1. A description of the sector 4.0

Three previous industrial revolutions—mechanization using water and steam power, mass production using assembly lines, and automation using computers and information technology—have all led to changes in manufacturing practices.

Currently, the Fourth Industrial Revolution is being put into practice. This is also referred to as "Industry 4.0," and it is characterized by the industry's utilization of information and communication technology. It is based on developments from the Third Industrial Revolution. A network connection enhances computer-based production systems, giving them a virtual twin on the Internet. These permit the generation of data about themselves as well as communication with other systems. This is the subsequent stage of production automation. All systems are interconnected, creating "cyber-physical production systems" and "smart factories," where people, components, and production systems communicate across a network and where production is essentially autonomous. Industry 4.0 has the ability to bring about some astonishing advancements in industrial environments when these enablers are coupled. Examples include machines that can recognize flaws and start maintenance procedures on their own or self-organized logistics that can adjust to unforeseen changes in production. It also has the power to change how people behave while working. Industry 4.0 has the potential to attract people into smarter networks, which could result in more productive working.

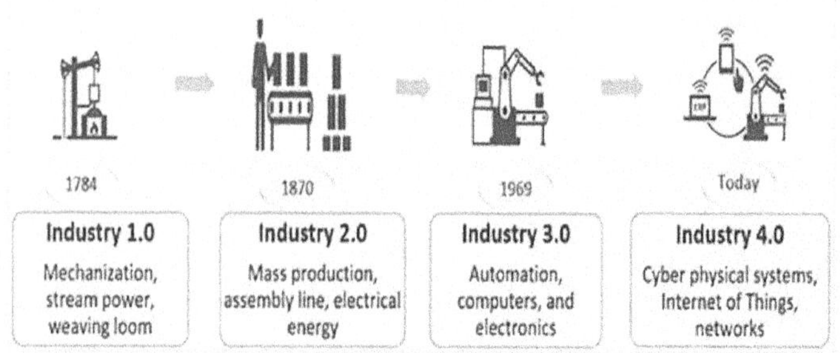

Figure 1. A visual representation of all industrial revolutions.

Digitization in the production environment offers more flexible ways to deliver the correct information to the right person at the right time. Thanks to the increasing use of digital devices both within factories and out in the field, maintenance employees may now obtain equipment documentation and service history more rapidly and at the point of use. Instead of wasting time hunting for technical information, maintenance professionals would rather spend their time addressing problems.

2.2. Definition of industry 4.0

The fourth industrial revolution, or "Industry 4.0," is the cyber-physical transformation of manufacturing. It is a concept that was developed by a group of experts from several fields including business, politics, and academia as part of an effort to integrate all manufacturing industry processes to attain sustainability. The phrase "Industry 4.0" refers to a government program in Germany that promotes networked manufacturing and a digital convergence of business, industry, and other operations as per *Kagermann, et al.*

Operations and manufacturing will essentially become more cost-effective and efficient as a result of Industry 4.0. These are completed by the straightforward exchange of information and the integrated control of industrial products and equipment, which operate in interoperability in a synchronized and intelligent manner.

The Fourth Industrial Revolution theorizes that the 21st century would see fast change in technology, industries, and societal patterns and processes because of growing interconnectedness and intelligent automation. Industry 4.0, which is distinguished by a few features of new technologies, is one of the most crucial ideas in the development of global industry and the global economy, according to Schwab. He emphasizes that the advancement of technology is having a significant impact on the development plans of industries, economies, and governments The term "industry 4.0" also refers to a social, political, and economic transition from the late 1990s and early 2000s to digital age to an embedded connection period characterized by extensive technological use.

The majority of the academics believed that Cyber-Physical Systems (CPS), Internet of Things (IoT), Industrial Internet, and other subjects were a component of Industry 4.0, in accordance with the ideas presented above. The cost and profitability of recently developed high-tech information and intelligent services was another topic heavily stressed by several authors in their works. Industry 4.0 was initially primarily focused on the industrial manufacturing sector, but numerous industries, including the automotive, engineering, chemical, and electronics industries, are increasingly adopting it. In order to improve the transformation of complete value chains of goods life cycles while creating novel products in manufacturing, Industry 4.0 is combining current concepts into a distinct value chain. This involves connecting systems and objects that are already in existence.

The fourth industrial revolution is the vision or scenario of a future production process that is characterized by new levels of controlling, organizing, and transforming the entire value chain with the life cycle of products through three types of effective integration: horizontal, vertical, and end-to-end engineering integration. Industry 4.0 results in increased productivity and flexibility, as well as cost optimization and reduction. The Internet of Things (IoT), cloud computing, additive manufacturing, artificial intelligence, AR, VR and other technologies are then brought together to create dynamic, real-time optimized, and self-organizing cross-company value networks. The futuristic Industry 4.0 concept relies on each of these elements, and they are all essential.

2.3. Industry 4.0 components and key enabling technologies

Industry 4.0 is a complex technical pattern that emphasizes the possibilities for integrating all the parts of a value-adding system through connection, integration, and industrial digitalization. This strategy takes into account digital manufacturing technology, network communication technology, computer technology, and automation technology. Industry 4.0 technological advancements are fusing human and machine agents, materials, products, industrial systems, and processes, erasing the distinction between the digital and physical worlds. Rapid technological advancements are made possible by Industry 4.0, but the fourth industrial revolution that is about to occur is largely being shaped by the technical incorporation of Cyber-Physical Systems into manufacturing processes as well as the use of the Internet of Things and Services in industrial processes. Each important technology driver for Industry 4.0 is briefly described in this section.

A. The Internet of Things (IoT)

The Internet of Things (IoT) connects the physical and digital worlds and allows for ubiquitous connections between computers and people. It has a wide range of purposes, roles, and facilities in daily life and across many fields. Additionally, Industry 4.0 is really ignited by IoT, more specifically the industrial Internet of things (IIoT). Industry 4.0 combines cutting-edge advancements like CPS, M2M connectivity, and IoT with traditional business and production procedures. The industrial sector is then transformed into smart firms by implementing self-customization, self-management, self-optimization, and self-cognition.

Smart factories are mostly dependent on the Internet of Things (IoT). Sensors on the production floor give the machines the ability to link to other web-enabled equipment by containing an IP address. Large volumes of useful data can be gathered, processed, and distributed thanks to the automation and interconnection of the world.

B. Cloud Computing

A key component of any Industry 4.0 plan is cloud computing. The connectivity and integration of engineering, supply chain, production, sales and distribution, and service are necessary for the full realization of smart manufacturing. The cloud makes that feasible. Additionally, the cloud can be used to process the normally vast amount of data being stored and evaluated more quickly and affordably. For small- and medium-sized manufacturers who can appropriately assess their demands and scale as their firm grows, cloud computing can significantly lower startup costs.

C. Machine learning and Artificial Intelligence

Artificial Intelligence and machine learning can produce insights that give operations and business processes visibility, predictability, and automation. For instance, industrial equipment frequently malfunctions when a product is being produced. Businesses can do machine learning-based predictive maintenance using data gathered from these assets, increasing uptime and efficiency.

Manufacturing firms can fully benefit from the abundance of information created not just on the factory floor but also across all of their business units, as well as from partners and outside sources, thanks to AI and machine learning.

The big data created by businesses is referred to as "industrial big data" in Industry 4.0. Businesses create this data by using cyber-based data, cloud-based data, data from IoT devices and security cameras, human-computer interfaces, mobile devices, and smart sensors. After that, the collected data can either be directly kept in the industry's database for later use or transmitted to the cloud for more sophisticated processing and analysis *(Yan et al., 2017)*. In light of this, big data and Industry 4.0 can transform industrial processes in order to reduce resource consumption and increase automation and process optimization, ultimately leading to sustainable development *(Bettencourt, 2014; Oliveira, 2019; Wu et al., 2016; Zhang et al., 2020)*.

2.4. Impact of Industry 4.0 on various sectors

Businesses, industries, and nations all rely heavily on innovation and scientific advancement. As a result of Industry 4.0 which will fundamentally alter industrial systems in terms of design, processes, operations, and services, societies will face new difficulties as well as advancements. Deep changes could be brought about by Industry 4.0 in a number of disciplines outside of the industrial sector. Six categories can be used to categorize its influence and effects: The industry sector is listed first, followed by goods and services, business models, entrepreneurship, and market competitiveness, national economies, the workplace, and skills development.

A. The impact of industry 4.0 on the industrial sector

The effects of Industry 4.0 will be felt most keenly in the business sector. With the advent of this new industrial paradigm, manufacturing will move toward a decentralized, digitalized vision where production elements may operate independently, initiate processes, and adjust to environmental changes.

The manufacturing sector in the United States has reached a turning point where robotization can increase employment and labor productivity of workers while also stimulating further growth of their education levels, according to *ROJKO, et al. (2020),* who used the vector autoregression model forecast for data from the manufacturing sector over the period (2008–2018). They came to the conclusion that there is a major impact of the change to Industry 4.0 on the rising demand for new knowledge and skills in order to increase productivity. As a result, as the Industry 4.0 era has begun, predicted growths of examined production indicators suggest that the negative effects of robotization in the recent past were just temporary.

2.5. Driving forces behind Industry 4.0

In addition to comprehending the idea of Industry 4.0, it's critical to talk about the elements that might influence businesses to adopt this strategy. Global shifts over time have created a networked civilization that affects both business and personal lives. They have also led to a number of adjustments for businesses engaged in manufacturing. According to *Kaivo-*

oja et al an omnipresent knowledge society with autonomous and intelligent devices is inevitable. In many modern cultures, particularly Western Europe, it is crucial to solve societal concerns. These difficulties include a smaller workforce due to an aging population and society. By creating and using new technology, they can be solved.

A. Business model innovation and sustainability

Industry 4.0 might potentially cause fundamental adjustments to current business paradigms, opening up fresh opportunities for value creation. These adjustments are anticipated to modify existing value chains and produce altogether new business models that permit greater consumer involvement. Industry 4.0 has an impact on three aspects of manufacturing SMEs: value creation, value capture, and value offer, according to *Müller et al. (2018)*. According to *Prem (2015)*, channels will become more digitalized as products and services become more and more digital. Customer interactions may evolve as a result, and product and service design innovation may rise. Thus, Industry 4.0 can be viewed as a fundamental pillar supporting the competitiveness of manufacturing firms in the future.

3. Barriers to Industry 4.0 implementation
A. Financial limitations

For the implementation of Industry 4.0 techniques, there are also some daunting opposing forces and obstacles. These challenges can be grouped into the following business categories: first, financial limitations. The implementation of Industry 4.0 presents significant financial challenges in terms of creating cutting-edge modern infrastructure and long-lasting process enhancements.

B. Technical expertise

Second, the primary focus that affects the amount of investment is the target organization's technical proficiency. On the other hand, the economic perspective is still in its infancy; a significant problem for adopting Industry 4.0 is a lack of transparency about cost-benefit analysis and financial returns on digital investments.

3.1. Challenges of Digital Marketing in Industry 4.0

The improved business offerings that come with this investment, such as higher product quality, more business continuity, increased productivity, and a stronger position above the competition, will be promoted with the use of strategic online and offline advertising. Of course, staying ahead of the competition is essential to gaining market share, and Industry 4.0, coupled with effective sales and marketing, can greatly aid in doing so.

In essence, Industry 4.0 transforms manufacturers into digital businesses. Industry 4.0 will take some time to spread throughout the firm. However, in order for a digital organization to be supported, you as marketers must evaluate your current digital infrastructure and how it will need to change.

A. Customization and personalization for modern consumers

Every marketer strives to improve customer experiences so that customers can tailor their interactions with their goods and services. People nowadays are more demanding than ever, and marketers alone won't be able to meet those demands unless they enlist the aid of digital equipment. Industry 4.0 is now required for every digital marketer to operate their firm in the competitive environment of today.

B.   Frequent misconfiguration faced by manufacturers

Though industry 4.0 is a great technical revolution in the digital market, it does have some challenges. And the first challenge is frequent misconfiguration which includes broken link or unstable link, non-reaching commands, network server or IP misconfigurations, noisy device causing traffic flood, etc. There might be many more frequent misconfigurations that have a huge impact on your business. So to solve this problem, you need to check the visibility of all assets and communications within your networks.

3.2. Exploring digital solutions for marketers

Three Industry 4.0 technologies have emerged in response to these altering client tastes and behaviors as well as the ways in which sales teams are developing appear to be becoming increasingly important at the find and shop stage:

A.   Use of Artificial Intelligence (IA)

Businesses are implementing AI technologies around their goods, services, and solutions to enable a natural-language Q&A conversation with customers. Online and through mobile apps, AI-driven platforms can gather data from various systems to generate recommendations based on a wide range of information about clients, services, and products, possibly making them smart and valued sales partners.

4.   Recommendation

For the majority of manufacturers, digital transformation probably involves significant change. While many see it as exciting and important, each also carries a variety of dangers and problems that can make this shift challenging. No problem is insurmountable, but everyone probably needs a well-thought-out plan and strategy to solve it.

Some manufacturers may place a greater emphasis on one stage of the client experience than others as they build new digital capabilities. Others might make general investments. There are doable measures that any manufacturers can take right now to address these issues and get going on this path, regardless of their focus or strategy. The recommendation to manufacturing executives is to set specific goals for themselves and their teams, including:

- Consider the ways a corporation or its channel partners might be mediated by a digitally first entry. This is typically a quick technique to spot vulnerable areas in the profit model as well as sources of latent value in customer relationships.

- Analyzing possible investments at the specific segment level can assist maximize

5. Conclusion

By discussing the crucial elements, traits, impacts on numerous dimensions, drivers, impediments, and other implementation issues of Industry 4.0, the fourth industrial revolution presents a hypothetical future production system, this study helps close the crucial gap. Industry 4.0 is an unavoidable transformation that encompasses many cutting-edge technologies, including sophisticated robots, IoT, cloud computing, RFID, cyber-physical systems, and smart factories. Numerous industries, including the automotive, shipping, aerospace, and energy sectors, are undergoing major transformations thanks to the Industry 4.0 paradigm. The development and incorporation of information and communication technology into business processes is what is meant by "industry 4.0." Organizations can benefit greatly from the capabilities or elements of Industry 4.0, including product customization, real-time data analysis, improved visibility, autonomous monitoring and control, dynamic product design and development, greater productivity, and competitiveness.

Organizations, industries, and nations all benefit greatly from innovation and technical progress. However, as interconnection and digital transformation progress, society will face new difficulties as a result of Industry 4.0, which will fundamentally alter how things are designed, manufactured, and operated. Industry 4.0 helps rethink traditional industrial processes by utilizing a number of cutting-edge tools and technology. The application of Industry 4.0 will have an impact across the entire value chain, improving production and engineering processes, product and service quality, and customer-organization relationships. Industry 4.0 also has a significant potential to bring about new business opportunities and economic benefits, change educational requirements, and transform the workplace. Industrial processes are being digitalized and connected (Industry 4.0), creating opportunities in all three dimensions of sustainability.

References

Bettencourt, L. M. (2014). The uses of big data in cities. *Big data*, *2*(1), 12-22.

Cao, B., Wang, X., Zhang, W., Song, H., & Lv, Z. (2020*)*. A many-objective optimization model of industrial internet of things based on private blockchain. *IEEE Network*, *34*(5), 78-83.

Finance, A. T. C. C. (2015). Industry 4.0 Challenges and solutions for the digital transformation and use of exponential technologies. *Finance, Audit Tax Consulting Corporate: Zurich, Swiss*, 1-12.

Kagermann, H., Helbig, J., Hellinger, A., & Wahlster, W. (2013). Securing the future of German manufacturing industry,

Recommendations for implementing the strategic initiative Industry 4.0: Final report 0f the Industry 4.0 working group. *Forschungsunion and Acatech National Academy of Science and Engineering.*

Khan, S., Ali, S. and Singh, R. (2022). Determinants of Remanufacturing Adoption for Circular Economy: A Causal Relationship Evaluation Framework, *Applied System Innovation,* 5(4), 62. https://doi.org/10.3390/asi5040062.

Khan, S., Singh, R. and Kirti. (2021). Critical Factors for Blockchain Technology Implementation: A Supply Chain Perspective, *Journal of Industrial Integration and Management,* 2150011. https://doi.org/10.1142/s2424862221500111.

Khan, S., Singh, R., Haleem, A., Dsilva, J. and Ali, S. (2022). Exploration of Critical Success Factors of Logistics 4.0: A DEMATEL Approach, *Logistics,* 6(1), 13. https://doi.org/10.3390/logistics6010013.

Müller, J. M., Buliga, O., & Voigt, K. I. (2018). Fortune favors the prepared: How SMEs approach business model innovations in Industry 4.0. *Technological Forecasting and Social Change*, *132*, 2-17.

Pachar, S., Singh, R. and Wahid, M. (2021). Implication of Renewable Energy in Sustainable Development in India: Future Strategy, *IOP Conference Series: Material Science and Engineering,* 1149(1), 012020. https://doi.org/10.1088/1757-899x/1149/1/012020.

Pachar, S., Singh, R.(2021). Role of Sustainable development goals and corporate social responsibility in India's growth: opportunities and challenges, *Empirical Economics Letters,* 20(2), 277-281.

Prem, E. (2015). A digital transformation business model for innovation. *The International Society for Professional Innovation Management (ISPIM)*.

Reiman, A., Kaivo-oja, J., Parviainen, E., Takala, E. P., & Lauraeus, T. (2021). Human factors and ergonomics in manufacturing in the industry 4.0 context–A scoping review. *Technology in Society*, *65*, 101572.Rojko, K. (2020). Sustainable industry robotization. *Innovative Issues and Approaches in Social Sciences*, *13*(2), 1855-0541.

Singh R. (2019). Issues & Challenges of Indian Education System in Current Scenario, International J. for Innovative Engineering and Management Research, 8(2):2456 – 5083.

Singh, R et al. (2022). Quality 4.0 in Healthcare: Application of the EFQM Excellence Mode. *Empirical Economics Letters*, 21(2), 1-19.

Singh, R. (2018). The Cause of Unemployment in Current Market Scenario, *Vivechan International Journal of Research*, 9(1), 86-81.

Singh, R., DSilva, J. and Kumar, R. S. (2021). Modelling the CSR Initiatives on Firm Performance: A Context of Emerging Economies, *Empirical Economic Letters,* 20 (3), 221-228.

Singh, R., Dsilva, J., Centobelli, P. and Tripathi, V. (2021). A review on Sustainable HRM: A study evaluating Sustainability for organisational development, The Empirical Economics Letters, 20(2), 1-10.

Singh, R., Khan, S. and Dsilva, J. (2022). A framework for assessment of critical factor for circular economy practice implementation, *Journal of Modelling in Management*, https://doi.org/10.1108/jm2-06-2021-0145.

Singh, S, Singh, R, Shandilya, T and Kumar, R.S. (2021). Digital security issues in emerging technology management, *Empirical Economics Letters,* 20(5), 205-213.

Umachandran, K., Corte, V. D., Amuthalakshmi, P., Ferdinand-James, D., Said, M. M. T., Sawicka, B., & Jurcic, I. (2019). Designing Learning-Skills towards Industry 4.0. *World. Journal on Educational Technology,11* (2), 12-23.

Wang, S., Wan, J., Zhang, D., Li, D., & Zhang, C. (2016). Towards smart factory for industry 4.0: a self-organized multi-agent system with big data based feedback and coordination. *Computer networks*, *101*, 158-168.

Weber, L. (2009). Marketing to the social web: How digital customer communities build your business (2nd ed.). John Wiley & Sons.

Witkowski, K. (2017). Internet of things, big data, industry 4.0– innovative solutions in logistics and supply chains management. *Procedia engineering*, *182*, 763-769.

Yan, J., Meng, Y., Lu, L., & Li, L. (2017). Industrial big data in an industry 4.0 environment: Challenges, schemes, and applications for predictive maintenance. *IEEE Access*, *5*, 23484-23491.

Zhou, K., Liu, T., & Zhou, L. (2015). Industry 4.0: Towards future industrial opportunities and challenges. *IEEE Access,* 2147-2152.

Chapter 13
Talent Analytics and Human Resource Management 4.0: Challenges and Remedies

Lama Blaique[1] Jacinta Dsilva[2]

[1]American University in Dubai (AUD), UAE

[2]SEE Institute, Sustainable City, Dubai-UAE

Abstract:

Over the past decade, the use of big data has been on the rise reasons being the increasing popularity of companies' usage of big data, such as the cost of storing and producing the data. With increasing literature indicating a positive impact of the latter on organizations, recent research is calling to understand how big data and its related analytical techniques can support human resource functions. Talent analytics (TA) is a sub-category of business analytics that uses methodologies to analyze patterns among employee data to efficiently manage the workforce and advance change including career progression. Despite the promising benefits of TA scholars call for additional research on areas related to TA. Therefore, the purpose of this chapter is twofold. First, to discuss the challenges HR managers face when dealing with talent analytics. Second, to offer practical solutions that may facilitate the efficient use of talent analytics.

Keywords: Big Data, Business Analytics, Talent Analytics, Industry 4.0, Human Resources

1. Introduction:

Over the past decades, the use of big data, big amounts of structured and unstructured data that is the result of routine activities by the organizations, has been on the rise. Several reasons can be attributed to the increasing popularity of company's usage of big data such as the cost of storing and producing the data. Due to this heighted interest from organizations, scholars started to explore the consequences of using big data on organizations and their performances. With increasing research indicating a positive impact of the latter organizations, recent research is calling for attempts to understand how big data and its related analytical techniques such as talent analytics, can support human resource functions within organizations. Talent analytics is a sub-category of business analytics that employs methodologies to analyze patterns among employee data to efficiently manage the workforce and advance change.

Despite the promising benefits of talent analytics presented in the literature, scholars call for additional research on several areas related to talent analytics such as quality of the data, talent analytics functions, and the relationship between business performance and talent analytics.

Therefore, the chapter focus is twofold. First, to discuss the challenges HR managers face when dealing with talent analytics. Second, to offer practical solutions that may facilitate efficient use of talent analytics. The chapter structure is as follows: section one - the concept of big data and discussion on talent analytics. Section two - the impact of talent analytics on organizational performance is discussed and further the challenges faced by HR managers in using talent analytics. Finally, offering solutions and practical recommendations that will aid senior management and HR experts on effectively employing talent analytics.

1.1 Big Data:

Big data was declared a major factor in productivity, competition, and innovation in 2011. Big data can be defined using four Vs (volume, variety, velocity, and value). Volume refers to the huge amount of data created, and it pertains to the size and scale of data sets. Variety pertains to the various forms of data within a dataset such as structured, semi and unstructured data. Velocity refers to the speed such as batch, near-real time, and streaming of data processing. Veracity relates to the data quality whether it is uncertain or imprecise. For example, IBM estimates that imprecise data costs the US economy around \$3.1 trillion annually. Because we are witnessing an increase in various sources and kinds of data, precision and trust are becoming harder to attain in big data analytics. Finally, value refers to the context and usefulness of data in decision making (Court, 2015).

Most organizations use databases to store complicated data. Such databases usually are cloud-based and are effective in producing reports and visual data using employee details. Big data analytics explain the method of analyzing large databases to identify patterns, undiscovered correlations, and other information that could not be analyzed in the past. Based on the big data's four Vs, analytical techniques must be reconsidered to surpass limitations on processing data relevant to time and space. Thus, opportunities for using big data are increasing in the modern world of digital data. The Big Data Market size was valued at USD 162.6 billion in 2021 and is projected to grow 273.4 USD billion by 2026. Technology advancement has enabled data analytics techniques such as ML, data mining, and CI that can minimize big problems, enhance decision making, decrease costs and foster efficient processing (Wang et al., 2015).

1.2 Talent Analytics:

Analytics as a term is gaining popularity since the big data concept is attracting attention in the corporate world. While many use the terms interchangeably, big data and analytics are very different terms. Analytics pertains to the methods that facilitate analysis of big data stored by an organization. INFORMS which is a Certified Analytics Professional, presents three types of analysis, namely descriptive, predictive and prescriptive analytics. Talent management (TM) is defined as the organized use of human resource management (HRM) activities to attract, find and retain people who are deemed talented (Meyers and van Woerkom, 2014). The word "talented" refers to potential employees who fill key positions within the organization. TM approach indicates that all individuals are talented whereby strategic goals can be improved by focusing on positive attributes and talents within employees. An effective workforce pipeline is the foundation for organizational success and stronger economies (CIDP, 2013). Some scholars indicate that TA enables the creation of the "perfect employee model" whereby the organization can evaluate factors that advance employee success and build qualification templates accordingly. Initially, the resulting models are utilized to identify potential candidates and therefore advance better decision making. After identifying and attracting the right individuals, organizations create development and advancement schemes (Furst, 2017). Under analytical HR, TA is used to determine performance drivers within each department and estimate their overall organizational performance. The type of TA used for workforce forecast facilitates prediction of different workforce schemes and their impact on organizational performance. TA also helps make decisions related to staffing through talent supply chain and its related mechanisms. TA is used to discover potential candidates especially for vacancies that require rare skillsets. TA also aids in evoking any unconscious bias from the recruitment process.

Training and development are a crucial activity provided by the HR department. Analytics-based dashboards are used to create personalized training plans based on educational background, skillset, and job requirements. In addition, it generates data used to calculate return on the training investment. TA provides tools that can connect employee performance management and compensation. The reports produced can map organizational performance to either individuals or teams. The data aid management in their decisions to enhance staff retention in terms of focusing and enhancing motivation and policy design. Despite the increasing amount of literature on TA, it is still not clear what is intended by TA and how can it help HR professionals (Nocker and Sena, 2019).

1.3 TA and Organizational Performance:

Scholars indicate that analytics is an example of IT resources to enhance organizational performance. Yet the details on how this relationship may be strengthened is not very clear (Braganza et al., 2017). A considerable amount of research studied the impact of TA on organizational performance from the perspective of the resource-based view (RBV) (Verbeke and Yaan, 2013). Accordingly, organizations initially need to identify their competitive advantage and then recognize certain areas associated with analytics to leverage competitive advantage within the organization. In addition, analytics can be viewed as an intangible asset investment. Another group of researchers relied on different theoretical views to explore the relationship between TA and organizational performance. Aral et al. (2012) explain that organizations that utilize a mix of pay for performance compensation, human capital management (HCM) software and HR analytics tend to be productive since this combination enables managers to both align incentives and observe staff behavior. Using a longitudinal study their results indicate that organizations with this mixture of capabilities and resources were drastically more productive. Interestingly their study shows that TA alone did not enhance organizational performance but when combined with HCM software and pay for performance the HR analytics resulted in higher performance. Organizations that employ talented individuals and supply them with motivation and support are expected to perform better compared to employees that do not.

Despite the considerable amount of research indicating a positive impact of TA on organizational performance, some studies indicate that TA result in cost saving outcomes only and that their impact on performance tends to be restricted (Davenport et al., 2010). In the next section, we will discuss in more details the challenges faced by experts and professionals as well as several practical recommendations.

1.4 Challenges faced by HRM in implementing TA

Businesses in the 21st century are facing different challenges and at a very high speed. Therefore, the response mechanism must be thoroughly evaluated. The new strategy is to understand both the internal and external customers, which means evaluating employee treatment and how these employees retain customers. Organizations have great opportunities if they are willing to engage its HR, however, due to lack of foresight, poor HR leadership and investment in the HR, organizations fail to have a competitive advantage.

According to CIPD (2013), the first challenge has been that departments often perform in silos, this hampers efficient access to data. The root cause is the structural and hierarchical barriers developed due to the traditional functioning of businesses. This affects the entire organization since the exchange of data is either delayed or restricted. Systems incompatibility, safety-security, and IT skills issues may be present due to system silos. Another challenge is collecting a humungous amount of data from different sources and combining it into presenting meaningful and informative reports. These reports have an integral role to play in supporting crucial decision making, instead of manual reporting, which most of the times lead to human error and poor decision making. However, the challenge is data credibility and security for most of the businesses (Kishnani, 2019). Another roadblock is skill sets required for optimal usage of the technology. It is true that HR analytics has become an important source to achieve competitive advantage, however, the reality is that most of the HR professionals lack the analytical abilities to understand the trends in the market and this hampers the performance of the organization. It is, therefore, necessary that businesses invest in up-skilling the HR professionals to make them efficient to utilize the richness of HR analytics. A commonly discussed challenge is the lack of support from the management and skepticism on behalf of the team carrying the HR analytics process. The main aim of installing any technology is to have a return on investment (ROI). Organizations in general tend to tie up investments and performances and when the returns are poor it is often considered as not so useful technology. However, unless the inhibitions of the employees are resolved, the work culture is data driven and the managers are motivated to engage in evidence-based processes, it is very hard for any organization to compete in extreme conditions (Afzal, 2019).

2.   Practical Implications and Recommendations

HR managers are the brain behind the operation and can be crucial in making important decisions regarding important asset i.e., people in the organization. The following recommendations aim at supporting HR managers in implementing efficient TA in their organization. According to Ofori-Boateng (2020), HR professionals no longer must make decisions based on their gut feeling, instead they can utilize the available data and develop new processes with the help of analytics to make decisions. Going forward, this will reduce the cognitive biases which often are seen during performance appraisal phase, wherein, managers end up providing mediocre rating to most of the employees due to the perception about each employee rather than considering the actual performance. TA can reduce this halo effect by providing detailed analysis of an employee's performance and eventually assists managers in reducing bias. Such radical changes can improve the employee work attitude and management and employee relationship. Recognition is a major motivator for higher performance among employees. In a traditional setup, the manager always notices the best performer and reward that person. This leads to demotivating other employees and leads to a mediocrity culture and high turnover. On the other hand, if an organization uses performance-based targets, the employees will be evaluated based on their performance leading to challenge-based mindset and higher performance achieving competitive advantage (Collings et al., 2018). HRM is a complete process which involves people management and performs several functions. HR managers liaise with both the management and employees to reduce any conflicts. However, the HR manager functions have increased due to change in work patterns, flexi-time and change employee attitudes. Thus, TA supports in developing advanced systems and processes for example, by utilizing data analytics when providing promotions, less time consuming and clarity on the yardsticks used for promotion, raise, transfer or even demotion (Ofori-Boateng, 2020). To summarize, TA offers a way to demonstrate the value created by HRM initiatives, thereby making the organization more credible and capable of surviving during extreme times.

In recommendation, it is imperative that HR managers embrace the change due to the technological advancement and understand that this change is inevitable. Managers should work toward change rather than against it. Therefore,

1.   Unless managers and employees work together to develop themselves it is going to be challenging to harvest the benefits of TA and enhance performance.

2.   HR professionals and managers should aid in employee skill and knowledge development. It is necessary to understand that basic computer skills are not going to be helpful, employees should be trained to develop their analytical skills across several ranges of TA software and applications.

3.   To build a TA task force since some organizations prefer to have a separate analytics team that includes tasks such as producing dashboards as well as act as service providers to other departments in reducing data silos. Such team can also assist HR teams in designing evidence-based solutions which can improve organizational performance.

4.   HR managers should be mindful of the ethical use of data since most of the information gathered in the HR department is about employees' personal details, salary related information and other confidential matter. Thus, such information is considered sensitive in nature and should be protected. One good example is General Data Protection Regulation (GDPR) developed by EU law for data protection purposes, which limits the unnecessary intrusion of any person into an employee's personal data and restricts collection of data that is not meant to be collected. It also makes sure that the data collected is used for the right purpose for which it has been collected. This practice can be implemented in every organization to protect the confidentiality of employee data.

3.   Conclusion:

This chapter provides an overview of the several functions of TA. It also draws on the importance of TA in terms of enhancing organizational performance. It is important to note that the literature on TA is limited in terms of research, however, more recent research has been focusing on discussing the challenges in adopting TA (Huselid,2018). Unfortunately, due to the continuing confusion about what is involved in TA implementation as well as the lack of clarity on the aspects that prevent its adoption by organizations, the advancement of the TA field and the establishment of widely accepted practices are moving at a slow pace (Fernandez and Gallardo, 2020). Therefore, the above chapter focuses on highlighting some of the challenges that hinders the successful implementation of TA. The final section of the chapter provides recommendations that will assist HR managers in overcoming some of these challenges. Our recommendations call to examine the process of talent analytics as part of the regular HR procedure rather than seeing it as an obstacle within the organization's day-to-day operations.

References

Alexis, F. and Sturman, M. (2017). HR Metrics and Talent Analytics. In The Oxford Handbook of Talent Management. Edited by David G. Collings, Kamel Mellahi and Wayne F. Cascio. Oxford: Oxford University Press.

Aral, Brynjolfsson, and Wu. (2012). Three-way complementarities: Performance Pay, human resource analytics, and information technology. *Management Science,* 58, 913–31.

Afzal., M. (2019). HR Analytics: Challenges and prospects of indian IT Sector. *International*

Journal of Management, IT and Engineering, 9(7), 404–415.

Braganza, Brooks, Nepelski, Ali, and Moro. (2017). Resource management in big data initiatives: Processes and dynamic capabilities. *Journal of Business Research,* 70, 328–37.

Childe, J. (2017). Big data analytics and firm performance: Effects of dynamic capabilities. *Journal of Business Research* ,70, 356–65.

CIPD, *Learning and talent development*, (2013). *Chartered Institute of Personnel and Development*, London.

Collings, D. G., Scullion, H., & Caligiuri, P. M. (2018). Global Talent Management: An Introduction. In *Global talent management* (pp. 3-15). Routledge.

Court, D. (2015). Getting big impact from big data. *McKinsey Q*, 1,52–60.

Fernandez, V. and Gallardo-Gallardo, E. (2021). Tackling the HR digitalization challenge: key factors and barriers to HR analytics adoption. *Competitiveness Review*, 31(1), 162-187.

Furst, J. (2017). Where is big data the most effective? Using talent analytics can help shape a more productive and efficient workforce.

Jeanne, H., Craig, E., and Light, D. (2011). Talent and analytics: new approaches, higher ROI.

Journal of Business Strategy, 32, 4–13.

Kishnani, N. (2019). Talent Analytics for Organizations of 21st Century. *SSRN Electronic*

Journal.

Meyers, M.C., & Van Woerkom, M. (2014). The influence of underlying philosophies on talent management: Theory, implications for practice, and research agenda. *Journal of World Business*,

49(2), 192-203.

Ofori-Boateng, C. (2020). Council Post: Using Data Analytics to Improve Your HR

Management. *Forbes*.

Verbeke, A., & Yuan, W. (2013). The drivers of multinational enterprise subsidiary entrepreneurship in China: A new resource-based view perspective. *Journal of Management Studies*, 50(2), 236–58.

Wang, X., & Huang, J.Z. (2015). Editorial: Uncertainty in learning from big data. *Fuzzy Sets Syst*, 258(1), 1–4.

Khan, S., Ali, S. and Singh, R. (2022). Determinants of Remanufacturing Adoption for Circular Economy: A Causal Relationship Evaluation Framework, *Applied System Innovation,* 5(4), 62. https://doi.org/10.3390/asi5040062.

Pachar, S., Singh, R. and Wahid, M. (2021). Implication of Renewable Energy in Sustainable Development in India: Future Strategy, *IOP Conference Series: Material Science and Engineering,* 1149(1), 012020. https://doi.org/10.1088/1757-899x/1149/1/012020.

Pachar, S., Singh, R. (2021). Role of Sustainable development goals and corporate social responsibility in India's growth: opportunities and challenges, *Empirical Economics Letters*, 20(2), 277-281.

Singh, R et al. (2022). Quality 4.0 in Healthcare: Application of the EFQM Excellence Mode. *Empirical Economics Letters,* 21(2), 1-19.

Singh, R., DSilva, J. and Kumar, R. S. (2021). Modelling the CSR Initiatives on Firm Performance: A Context of Emerging Economies, *Empirical Economic Letters,* 20 (3), 221-228.

Singh, R., Dsilva, J., Centobelli, P. and Tripathi, V. (2021). A review on Sustainable HRM: A study evaluating Sustainability for organisational development, The Empirical Economics Letters, 20(2), 1-10.

Singh, R., Khan, S. and Dsilva, J. (2022). A framework for assessment of critical factor for circular economy practice implementation, *Journal of Modelling in Management*, https://doi.org/10.1108/jm2-06-2021-0145.

Singh, S, Singh, R, Shandilya, T and Kumar, R.S. (2021). Digital security issues in emerging technology management, *Empirical Economics Letters,* 20(5), 205-213.

Chapter 14
Being Realistic with the Digital Marketing Analytics: Conversion Optimization Rate

Kavita Chauhan[1], Saurabh Singh[2]

[1]Department of Management Studies, Jamia Millia Islamia, Delhi

[2]Shaheed Bhagat Singh College, University of Delhi, India

1: Introduction:

The new era of digital business has made the organisations realise that in order to survive they need to walk out of the brick and motor environment and make its presence apparent on the virtual platform. One of the most commonly used medium till date for which is websites. The chapter attempt to highlight the concept of Conversion Rate Optimization as the mere presence on the virtual platform via website may fail to serve the purpose as it not the visitor count that generate business in every case rather who among those visitors have been converted to the customer is what ultimately matters in terms of revenue generation. Thus, the chapter starts from building the base of CRO and move towards its objectives, advantages, implications, key aspects and practices to provide an overall clarity of the concept.

2: Understanding Conversion Rate optimization (CRO):

The VUCA culture of the 21st century is characterized by rigid online traffic. It's difficult to persuade visitors to follow through your conversion funnel at their first try, while their likelihood of returning to yield the action is fairly low. To simply put, here is where the organisation has lost their opportunity. An optimum strategy in improving our chances to get more conversions is to run effective campaigns for conversion rate optimisation. The goal conversion rate optimisation actualises is increasing the probability that a visitor converts via the aforementioned page. Another bird killed by this stone is enhancement of user experience at the web-page to condition user behaviour.

CRO is linked to the process of rocketing the fraction of people that visit a particular website. The desired outcomes include activities of buying a product, adding to the basket, signing up for a service, clicking a link or a pop-up on a web-page.

Standard definitions of CRO, like the one above, place a strong emphasis on conversion rates, averages, and benchmarks. This emphasis on numbers has the drawback of making you tend to forget about the individuals who carried out those conversions when you stare at spreadsheets full of conversion data points and actions.

Therefore, a more comprehensive and user-centric approach to CRO may be described as a process that focuses on understanding what inspires, discourages, and persuades the organization's target audience.

The second definition is thought to be more comprehensive because conversion is the final phase and should therefore receive the most attention, despite the fact that a lot occurs before that. Organizations and professionals should be aware of the fact that visitors come to your website for a variety of DRIVERS but leave due to a variety of BARRIERS. The figure below represents the inverse correlation of the drivers and the obstacles as well as the insight that must be acknowledged and looked upon by the organisation for further actions.

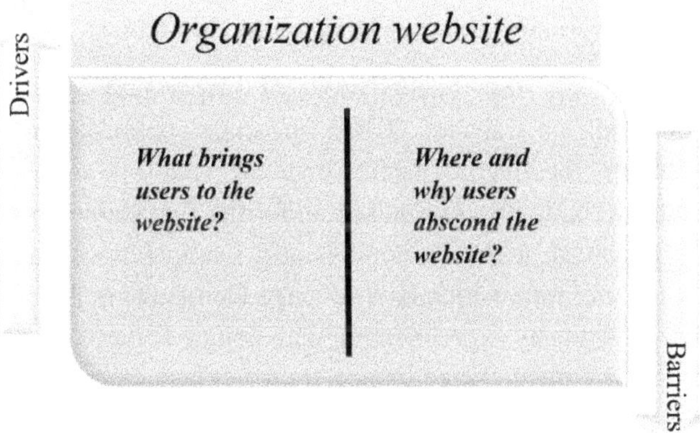

2.1: What good CRO does to an Organisation?

Nowadays, businesses use CRM software and packages, which frequently prompts them to question the need for CRO. It is important to note that the CRM software seeks to gather information from individuals who have completed a transaction and provided some credentials at the site, but what about those site users who browsed the page, made a few clicks, and then departed without providing any personal information? In such a scenario, the CRO's function becomes increasingly clear. As CRO helps organisations understand and record the whys and how's of site visitors' behaviour, it enables them to maximise the functionality of their websites. The harsh reality is that until a website is properly experimented with and maintained, it will never operate at its full capacity. The CRO application assists the organisation in two key areas, assisting it in attaining the goals established, namely:

- Improving advertising, and

- Marketing ROI

A well-established and well-thought-out CRO application predominantly and totally based on robust evaluation that can pass a protracted manner in augmenting go back on nearly all of your advertising and marketing sports through:

- Improving the quality/pace of experiments run for organisation's website: CRO permits organisations to investigate the overall performance of your online website through walking checks and search for the fine viable versions which promise and aids conversions. Organizations can run tests to determine which landing page elements are producing the best results by experimenting with unique features, and they can also use the gathered data as a crucial benchmark for their subsequent round of tests and experiments.

- Better sales with the equal traffic/incremental commercial enterprise returns: One of the top advantages of walking a CRO marketing campaign is that each alternate you enforce for your website online, which subsequently will increase your conversions, is an incremental win to your commercial enterprise.

3: Channel Buyer Behaviour

Not every problem you encounter when attempting to boost conversions has a clear resolution, is quantifiable, and is backed by hard evidence. It's true that there are times when a clear error prohibits 80% of your users from taking a particular action, and correcting that one defect would save your entire company. There are also instances where your website functions properly but doesn't generate any conversions from users. When this happens, you must go beyond the data you already have to understand why; in other words, you must prioritise your users.

4: CRO Implications for e-commerce business:

For some time, e-Commerce firms have been growing and intensifying. The list may include well-known companies like Amazon, Flipkart, Blinkit, and many others. Users of such websites have been observed to suspend their shopping carts or abandon them without finishing their purchases, which has no positive impact on organisation. Shopping cart abandonment is one of the most challenging circumstances for eCommerce firms, costing them billions of dollars in lost revenue every year.

- Therefore, it's deemed crucial to create an eCommerce website that is user-friendly, has a great design, excellent products, and affordable shipping that not only addresses the cart abandonment issue but also other drop-off issues like a confusing price process, losing basic information, etc.

- Common motives why human beings depart a domain are as follows:

o Distractions: Too many pop-united states or bureaucracy to fill can distract your customers.

o Difficulty of checkout: The website might not provide a pleasant test-out option, which might also additionally complicate the buying efforts of first-time users.

o Hidden charges: Most site visitors get intimidated through hidden charges consisting of extra transport charges, different taxes, and extra.

Running a CRO marketing campaign makes it easier to identify and address such bottleneck issues, which significantly helps to increase the conversion rate of the website online.

Digital advertising and marketing companies that offer many services to their clients, such as social media promotion, web content creation, logo development, etc., might present CRO options to those clients as a way to increase the visibility of their current traffic. This will not only help them attract more clients by providing a service in addition to their standard ones, but it will also enhance their overall business impact.

5: How to calculate conversion rate?

The number of conversions (desired actions taken) is divided by the total number of visits, and the resulting number is multiplied by 100 to produce the conversion rate as a percentage.

Conversion Rate = (Number of Conversion / Total Number of Visitors) * 100

For example, if your web page had 18 sales and 450 visitors last month, your conversion rate is 18 divided by 450 (0.04), multiplied by $100 = 4\%$.

5.1: What is the average conversion rate?

Each website, page, and target audience are unique. In any case, people do not disclose their conversion details publicly. Averages are useful as starting points for benchmarking, but what do they really have to do with an organization's website?

There isn't any true, conclusive business figure that one can rely on or compare themselves to with absolute certainty. It's not always the best way to think about conversion rate optimization to obsess over a mean percent figure and try to squeeze as many conversions as you can just to stay within it. Once more, you are better off focusing on developing a deep understanding of what really matters to people so that an organisation can offer it to them. Conversions will naturally follow.

6: Conversion optimization pleasant practices—and why they're dangerous:

Conversion price optimization steps:

Understanding the system: Multiple conversion price optimization frameworks exist that may successfully assist conversion price optimizers plan and execute optimization campaigns. CRO system may be divided into five stages:

Stage 1:

The studies phase – Identifying the regions of improvement. As a general rule, most business owners tend to copy CRO strategies that worked for other organisations because they believe they will also be successful. However, they fall short because neither each orange button nor each lengthy form page can fail.

Understanding what customers do (quantitative statistics) -The first and fundamental element to do is get familiarized with the basics.

-    Analyze how is your traffic doing?

Analytics enables decision-making that is entirely based on facts and data as opposed to gut feelings. There are various methods for obtaining statistics in the CRO system to understand your results. For instance, a business may obtain essential information from its online analytics tools, such as real-time data tracking, rise rate, incoming internet site visitor's sources, audience, demography, website behaviour, and many more. One of the best tools for obtaining precise quantitative data on what people are doing on your website is Google Analytics.

Stage 2:

How do web page capabilities form person conduct? See how specific features of a website are influencing person behaviour by utilising tourist behaviour evaluation tools such as heatmaps, consultation recordings, interview feedbacks, customer surveys, analytics, and internet promoter score, among others. For instance, you might discover that the search feature on your landing page generates more conversions than the featured product categories. Receiving such insights can greatly help you eliminate undesired skills and concentrate more on ones that convert clients more effectively.

Understanding Person Conduct (Qualitative Statistics)

Customer psychology usually lays down the essential floor policies for CRO factors to follow.

Two important factors that resource in knowledge patron psychology are:

1. Persuasion principles: People are incredibly susceptible to recommendations and cognitive biases. To give an example, an object becomes much more famous when it is known that it is one of hundreds, regardless of its actual value. An object becomes more valuable at the same time that it becomes rarer and more unique. To effectively establish your goals and create a CRO plan that boosts your business's earnings, it's crucial to comprehend human psychology.

Additionally, adding social proof in the form of reviews and testimonials to your landing page or somewhere appropriate will help your efforts. Social proofing encourages more conversions, according to the majority of online case studies!

2. Customer conduct: Studying the conduct of your audience offers a perception into "why they do what they do" over internet, and the way you may use this fact to construct a higher-changing internet site. There is number one approach to have a look at the conduct of your audience: Conducting assessments and taking in-man or woman interviews.

Performing evaluations and conducting in-person interviews: You can receive extensive information and insights on a variety of things by closely observing how your customers engage with your website in real-time. These can include the webpages users visit the most, the amount of time they spend on your website, the areas where they encounter the greatest difficulties, such as having trouble filling out forms, being unable to create passwords, experiencing charge drop-off, and much more.

Reading case studies and applying guidelines for behaviour: Numerous recent studies and case studies can be a great source of information about the collective psyche of your clients, which can then be used to improve the overall look and feel of your website and increase conversions. When you combine the two, you'll have a much more comprehensive understanding of how your customers are acting on your website.

Stage 3:

The prioritization phase – select an order Here, some of frameworks assist you to via the system. Of those, the P.I.E. framework formulated through Chris Goward at Wider Funnel is what we maximum recommend:

Potential

Find out the pages that are performing worst and can improve greatly.

Importance

Then narrow down by selecting the ones that have the most valuable traffic. Traffic is valuable when it's either costly (paid) or super relevant to your product offering.

Ease

Even when you have a final list of pages, it's important to realize that not all pages are easily optimized. A page, such as an eCommerce product listings page, may be technically complicated to start optimizing while another, such as your home page, may have too many stakeholders to please. It's important to go for the one that is easily optimized first and then move up the list.

Source: https://vwo.com/conversion-rate-optimization

Stage 4:

The purchasing section: Determining whether a special feature on our website may help produce increased conversions is one of the top reasons to do a test. For instance, you've decided to check the first 100 people who have visited your website online. You observe that forty of the hundred visitors changed at the variation you ran toward 20 at the original website. That's a 20% conversion rate as opposed to the meagre 10% on the original website. But does this mean you'll always get a guaranteed 20% conversion charge?

Most likely not, as the 100 visitors wouldn't represent a particularly good representation of the 10,000 visitors who pay a visit to your page online each day. Here, statistical significance is relevant!

Stage 5:

The segment on getting to know you as a tool to evaluate test results while here is the section when you come to your final judgments about your experiments, close the loop for conversion rate optimization and pay attention to all of the fresh information gathered for subsequent testing. Unfortunately, most optimizers only look at the test results to see if a variant became the dominant one or, if it failed, they go on to developing better hypotheses. However, as an optimizer, going deeper is significantly more important. Conversion rate optimization requires time, resources, and, if done correctly, analysis. To increase the likelihood that a potential customer who finds your website online through a search engine converts into a qualified lead or a paying customer, it is more than worth your time to become familiar with the core concepts and metrics of website conversion optimization.

There are several things you can do to increase your conversion rate, some of which include:

• Write engaging, clickable PPC ads that are incredibly relevant to the keyword or seek question and your intended target. The better, as these customers are much more likely to convert, if you're concentrating on high-reason mid-tail and long-tail keywords that indicate a searcher who's past due inside the buying cycle.

• Maintain a high level of relevancy between your ads and accompanying landing pages. Your landing page needs to fulfil the call to action in your advertisement and make it simple for the searcher to do that action, whether it's subscribing to a newsletter, downloading a white paper, or making a purchase.

• Test the layout of your landing page. Find the layout, copy, and colours that encourage the highest percentage of internet traffic to fill out your form, enter their information, or otherwise convert to a valuable lead or customer by doing A/B testing. Increasing PPC Conversions: Select the Correct Keywords First

• When you start thinking about conversion rate optimization, it can be tempting to play around with buttons, red tape, and other low-in-the-funnel design elements that could make or break the transaction. But keep in mind that attracting the right traffic to your website in the first place is a crucial component of conversion optimization: • A high number of visitors is useless if none of them convert.

• With seek marketing, growing your certified site visitor is an issue of bidding on and optimizing for the proper key phrases.

• Better keyword traffic data allows you to target the right customers more effectively when making decisions about your website and advertisement copy. Optimizing conversion rates and landing pages. The excellent quality of your individual landing pages could have a significant effect on conversion rates. Consider the scenario where a potential customer finds your website as a consequence of a certain search query. If the information and presentation on that page don't relate to what they were looking for or watching for to learn, they will return to their search, and you will lose that lead. And the undesirable results are not prevented there! Poorly constructed landing pages can also cause your Quality Score to plummet, which can then increase your cost per click and cost per action and lower your ad rank, making it more challenging to secure positions in Google's ad auction.

Common good practises for web page design include a few essential elements:

•   Create a headline that is compelling and relevant to your PPC keyword so that visitors will stay on the page and complete your desired action.

•   Concise, focused reproduction - The content of your website should clearly express what you are offering and speak directly to the keywords associated with that ad group. To prevent your reproduction from being too lengthy or overpowering, use bulleted lists.

•   Clickable, eye-catching call-to-action (CTA) - Make sure your CTA button is visually noticeable, appears clickable, and uses brief, gain-centred content.

•   User-friendly lead capture form - A top form has all the fields required to fulfil your offer, but not too many that potential clients are visually overloaded. When creating your form, be sure to give careful thought to the information that is absolutely necessary to capture.

•   Attractive standard design - Landing pages should be smooth and uncluttered to give potential clients a sense of reliability and professionalism. In order to prevent a confusing browsing experience for visitors, design should also be consistent with your logo.

Following these best practises will keep your landing pages relevant and high-quality, leading to a desired boost in both CRO and Quality Score.

However, there is one middle premise. One suggestion is frequently made and is generally true: spend time getting to know your customers and clients. Or, as we like to say around here at Hotjar, develop a client-centric way of life by obsessing over your clients and clients. They are the ones who keep track of numbers for your business and offer the answers you need to make it better. Focus on their goals and desired outcomes, learn as much as you can about their concerns and reluctances, and then respond in a way that addresses those. The most common way involves investing in knowledge, learning from your consumers, and using that knowledge to build an optimization strategy that continuously improves your business. Your brain, ears, eyes, and mouth are your best tools for understanding your customers, empathising with their experiences, drawing conclusions based on the facts, and ultimately making the changes that increase your product conversion rates.

7: Which are the best Conversion Rate Optimization Tools

By showing you how users interact with your website, CRO tools enable you to see how well it is performing. Simply told, these tools gather information about your visitors and website, assisting you in identifying the complex areas of your website that are causing users difficulty. There is a lot of nice CRO equipment available, and it's important to note that this equipment falls into 3 categories:

1. Web analytics CRO gear

2. Behavior analytics CRO gear

3. CRO trying out-gear

8: The CRO Cycle

You begin by deciding on your objectives. You compile pertinent information, evaluate it, and formulate a hypothesis. You develop your versions, apply technology, and evaluate your theory. The results are then analysed, which provides fresh perspectives and inspiration for fresh testing. Then, the procedure is repeated. The cycle of optimization and testing never ends. Not if you're doing it correctly, at least. Let's now discuss your actions at each phase of the cycle.

o   Establish Your Goals

An explicit purpose serves as the foundation of the process. Never forget that nothing can be optimised if your goals aren't clear. You need to be clear about your goals.

Say, for example, that you want to optimise your homepage. As an illustration, consider the homepage of Digital Marketer (DM). However, keep in mind that because homepages need to do so many various tasks—and because everyone has different priorities—they are one of the hardest pages to optimise. Qualified leads are what the sales staff is seeking for. The acquisition team is investigating methods for turning traffic into emails.

o   Your homepage serves as a welcome message.

o   The bottom line is that your homepage serves as a welcome message for new visitors. They are attempting to determine whether your company is pertinent to them, and if so, where they are now located and where they need to go.

Set one or more of the following three goal categories to make the most of this experience:

-   a short-term objective, such clicking or finishing an on-page form.

- a marketing objective, such as the number of leads or sales made.

- a long-term objective, such as improving lead quality, net revenue, average order value, or your long-term value.

As you can see from the DM homepage, the first type of objective, an immediate goal, is what we want to achieve most. We need folks to provide us with their email addresses.

However, the entire experience must be optimised, so let's take a look at the page that is displayed when a user clicks the "Get Your Invitation" button.

o They arrive at this page.

Finding the ideal product for fresh prospects is an optimization strategy for the long term.

This page benefits us on the front end and the back end, and it accomplishes the third kind of goal, a long-term goal. We can qualify people for the appropriate product, such as DM Lab or HQ, using the information we collect here. This is significant to us since it enables us to assess the calibre of the leads we are producing and directs new subscribers to the most appropriate offers.

o Obtain Information

After deciding on your objective, you must establish a starting point for your metrics. Record your existing number, your aspirational number (the number you want), and your user information for each. Before forming any assumptions, gather that information. Which takes us to the first optimization rule: don't make any assumptions. Everyone in your company, including you, has ideas about what attracts customers, what doesn't, and other things. However, those concepts are just presumptions. Never make choices based on presumptions. Try out your ideas and ask your audience what works for them.

o   What about your data source?

Visit Google Analytics to view site metrics. Utilize a technology like Tru Conversion for metrics on user activity. Use the information offered by your email service, such as ConvertKit, Infusionsoft, Aweber, etc., for client and email data. Check your payment processor, such as Stripe, Paypal, etc., for payment information. Reports like this one from Google Analytics, which provides information on the traffic to the page you're trying to optimise, reveal a variety of facts. Reports on user behaviour could resemble this one from Tru Conversion. It reveals areas where we may enhance the user experience by displaying where visitors are clicking while they are on the page.

o   Examine Data

The secret to CRO success is using the pertinent data you just collected to create impactful optimization efforts. Review your figures and ponder the following issues:

-   How well am I converting? (Is it also appropriate?) Use CRM or analytics data to uncover the solutions.

-   Why is my conversion rate declining? To determine this, use the data on user behaviour.

o   What is the cause or effect on my conversion rate?

You'll proceed to the following stage of the CRO process and create a hypothesis to provide a solution to this query. Create a hypothesis and all optimization starts with this. You can't optimise if you don't have a hypothesis since you won't know what you're aiming to get better at. You have your data and have determined the factors that are most likely affecting your conversion rates at this point in the process. You now need to hazard some assumptions as to how you might address the problem you've found. How do you form an assumption?

Making a statement with below components only takes a moment:

- The modification or strategy you want to try.
- Whom this modification is intended to affect.

Keep in mind that your hypothesis concerns your intention. You must be absolutely specific about the result you want to achieve. Additionally, you must confirm that it can be measured and will enhance your outcomes in a particular manner. Your data and your new hypothesis will be combined to produce the variations you'll test.

Remember that testing requires time, both to write and set up tests as well as to run them.

Although there is no restriction on the number of tests you may run on a website at any given time, you should still keep your test load low if your site receives little traffic since it takes too long to conduct a test and produce reliable findings.

In light of this, if your site receives little traffic, aim to run no more than 29 tests annually.

Therefore, you must choose the appropriate tests to execute. You must improve your capacity for locating and defending the page that you wish to optimise.

10: Concluding Remark:

Conversion Rate Optimization has evolved from identifying the value of website optimization to developing plans and strategies to enhance site performance, running A/B tests, and leveraging the results to strengthen marketing initiatives. It not only gives businesses the ability to comprehend how consumers use, think about, and perceive their brand and its products, but it also exposes them to a vast array of data that will help them develop their long-term business plans. CRO is "the" tool to make you stand out, not just another tool to improve your brand's online performance!

References:

Cheung, C. M. K., Zhu, L., Kwong, T., Chang, G., & Limayem, M. (2003). Online Consumer Behavior: A Review and Agenda for Future Research. 16th Bled ecommerce Conference, eTransformation, Bled, Sloveniahttps://www.zamaros.net/NACB%20READING%201 .pdf

Constantindes, E. (2002). The 4S Web-Marketing Mix model. *Electronic Commerce Research and Applications, 1*, 57-76. http://dx.doi.org/10.1016/S1567-4223

Constantindes, E. (2004). Influencing the online consumer's behavior: the Web experience. *Internet Research, 14*(2), 111-126. http://dx.doi.org/10.1108/10662240410530835

Constantinides, E., & Geurts, P. (2005). The Impact of Web Experience on Virtual buying Behaviour: An Empirical Study. *Journal of Customer Behaviour, 4*, 307-336.

http://dx.doi.org/10.1362/147539205775181249

Constantinides, E., Lorenzo-Romero, C., & Gomez, M. A. (2010). Effects of web experience on consumer choice: a multicultural approach. *Internet Research, 20*(2), 188-209. http://dx.doi.org/10.1108/10662241011032245

Conversion Rate Optimization. (n.d.). Retrieved from vwo.com: https://vwo.com/conversion-rate-optimization

Croxen-John, D., & Tonder, J. v. (2017). *E-Commerce Website Optimization: Why 95% of Your Website Visitors Don't Buy, and What You Can Do About it.* Kogan Page Ltd.

Cypress, B. (2018). Qualitative Research Methods: A Phenomenological Focus. *Dimensions of Critical Care Nursing, 37*(6), 302–309.

doi:10.1097/DCC.0000000000000322

Denscombe, M. (2017). *The Good Research Guide: For small-scale social research projects* (Vol. 6ed). London, England: Open University Press.

Econsultancy, & RedEye. (2017). *Conversion rate optimization report.*

Goward, C. (Director). (2016). INBOUND 2016: Chris Goward "Up Your Conversion Rate Optimization Program to Drive Leads" [Motion Picture]. Retrieved from https://www.youtube.com/watch?v=sNW5Sa2BnzA

Goward, C (2022). *Lift your sales and revenue with conversion optimization.* Retrieved from www.widerfunnel.com: https://www.widerfunnel.com/blog/how-to-prioritize-conversion-rate-optimization-tests-using-pie/

Hellesmark, K. (2018). *Koll på konverteringsoptimering?* Retrieved from Ateles Consulting: https://www.ateles.se/blog/koll-pa-konverteringsoptimering

Langdon, M. (2018). *A Brief History of Web Design.* Retrieved from Creativemms: https://creativemms.com/blog/a-brief-history-of-web-design/

Miikkulainen, R., Iscoe, N., Shagrin, A., Rapp, R., Nazari, S., McGrath, P., . . . Achkar, E. (2018). *Sentient Ascend: AI-Based Massively Multivariate Conversion Rate Optimization.* United States: AAAI Publications. Retrieved from https://www.aaai.org/ocs/index.php/AAAI/AAAI18/paper/view/17332

Phillips, J. (2016). *Ecommerce Analytics : Analyze and Improve the Impact of Your Digital Strategy.* New Jersey: Imprint Pearson FT Press.

Schlosser, A. E., White, T. B., & Lloyd, S. M. (2006). Converting Web Site Visitors into Buyers: How Web Site Investment Increases Consumer Trusting Beliefs and Online Purchase Intentions. *Journal of Marketing, 70*(2), 133-148. http://dx.doi.org/10.1509/jmkg.70.2.133

Shukairy, A. (2017). *What is Conversion Rate Optimization (CRO) and Why Is It Important?* Retrieved from www.invespcro.com: https://www.invespcro.com/blog/what-is-conversion-rate-optimization/

www.ingramcontent.com/pod-product-compliance
Ingram Content Group UK Ltd.
Pitfield, Milton Keynes, MK11 3LW, UK
UKHW021650190726
13853UKWH00001B/164